Youth, Culture and Photography

YOUTH QUESTIONS

Series Editors: PHILIP COHEN and ANGELA McROBBIE

This series sets out to question the ways in which youth has traditionally been defined by social scientists and policy-makers, by the caring professions and the mass media, as well as in 'common-sense' ideology. It explores some of the new directions in research and practice which are beginning to challenge existing patterns of knowledge and provision. Each book examines a particular aspect of the youth question in depth. All of them seek to connect their concerns to the major political and intellectual debates that are now taking place about the present crisis and future shape of our society. The series will be of interest to those who deal professionally with young people, especially those concerned with the development of socialist, feminist and anti-racist perspectives. But it is also aimed at students and general readers who want a lively and accessible introduction to some of the most awkward but important issues of our time.

Published

Inge Bates, John Clarke, Philip Cohen, Dan Finn, Robert Moore and Paul Willis
SCHOOLING FOR THE DOLE?
The New Vocationalism

Cynthia Cockburn
TWO-TRACK TRAINING
Sex Inequalities and the YTS

Andrew Dewdney and Martin Lister
YOUTH, CULTURE AND PHOTOGRAPHY

Dan Finn
TRAINING WITHOUT JOBS: NEW DEALS AND BROKEN PROMISES
From Raising the School-Leaving Age to the Youth Training Scheme

Angela McRobbie and Mica Nava (eds)
GENDER AND GENERATION

Forthcoming

Philip Cohen and Harwant Bains (eds)
MULTI-RACIST BRITAIN
New Directions in Theory and Practice

Philip Cohen and Graham Murdock (eds)
THE MAKING OF THE YOUTH QUESTION

Angela McRobbie (ed.)
RECORD COLLECTIONS
A Youth Reader

Kevin Robins and Frank Webster
NEW TECHNOLOGY AND EDUCATION

Youth, Culture and Photography

Andrew Dewdney
and
Martin Lister

MACMILLAN
EDUCATION

First published 1988

Published by
MACMILLAN EDUCATION LTD
Houndmills, Basingstoke, Hampshire RG21 2XS
and London
Companies and representatives
throughout the world

Typeset by TecSet Ltd, Wallington, Surrey

Printed in Hong Kong

ISBN 0–333–39179–9 (hardcover)
ISBN 0–333–39180–2 (paperback)

Contents

'. . . we cannot invent a form out of its time. It is necessary above all to approach the real *now* in one way or another – one sidedly, elliptically or not. The ethnographic account, for all its faults, records a crucial level of experience and through its very biases insists upon a level of human agency which is persistently overlooked or denied but which increases in importance all the time for other levels of the social whole.'

Paul Willis, *Learning to Labour* (Saxon House, 1977)

1

Youth, Photography and Education

Unless otherwise credited all photographs reproduced on the following pages were taken by young people working within the constituent projects of the Cockpit Arts Workshops (Dept of Cultural Studies) Schools Photography Project between 1979 and 1985.

About the book

This is not a 'how to do it manual', neither is it a comprehensive survey of photography in education. It is an account of work that has been carried out with young people in and out of school. In that sense we hope that it does provide models for practical work and guidelines for its development. It is also an account of the conditions in which that work was done and the ideas which supported it. We hope that this will be useful to others who may wish to initiate, organise and resource photographic projects with young people.

We have seen no point in proposing definitive methods and programmes for realising fixed aims and goals. There is no seamless picture of educational innovation in this book. We've tried instead to stay close to the real, uneven, and 'never settled' experience of working with resistant young people. We have done this at the expense of the greater apparent clarity and order that a more paradigmatic account might have allowed. We trust that this is, self-evidently, preferable.

The book integrates three themes: youth, photography, and education. At some points photography is widened to a more general view of cultural practice, and at others education is narrowed to 'schooling'. Throughout we are mindful of the way that young people are both consumers and makers of contem-

porary cultures while being restricted and even oppressed by a dominant culture's forms and institutions. We are especially concerned with the opportunities that working-class young people have for the expression and clarification of their experience. We look at the cultural and educational frameworks in which this can occur and the problematic relationship they can have with the everyday lives and futures of young people. These are questions which are continually raised or begged in the young people's work which this book also serves to present. Photography is the practical activity through which we have worked in schools and youth projects to explore these and other areas with young people. In doing this work we have tried never to assume the value and usefulness of photography. Photography has several cultural guises, social purposes, and institutional forms; we've tried to be vigilant and critical in respect of them and the interests of young people. Throughout the account we discuss how photography can be a popular and powerful means of expression for the young, how they variously understand it and meet it within their worlds, and where, almost despite its current forms of organisation, its educational potential lies.

The book is based on six years' practical work. We have worked mainly with fourth and fifth years in Inner London schools, or 14 to 16 year-olds in more informal community contexts. Some young people have continued to work with us beyond school-leaving age – which they interpret freely – and when unemployed or evading the clutches of the Youth Training Scheme. The majority have been male; about half Afro–Caribbean and about half white, although not necessarily of British parentage but also Italian, Spanish, Irish, Portugese, Greek Cypriot, and Turkish. Increasingly we have found Bangladeshi young people within our projects, and occasionally Vietnamese. We have worked with far fewer young women although the work of some of them is represented in the book. We can only explain this by reference to the fact that we are male and to the structural problem of a small agency which has to negotiate its work, in the first place, with secondary schools. Our projects are often offered as photography 'options' within the schools. Photography is a rather gendered practice and it is boys who mainly opt to do it. When we are invited to work with a timetabled group it is normally a predominantly male group, characterised as heavy, difficult or disruptive. Our interest and readiness to work with such groups only compounds the problem. On a wider basis, we often resource the work of girls' groups working with women tutors, but, in this book, we have not presumed to include this as our project. Overall it has been a boys' project.

Initial bearings: a critique of art education

In talking, or arguing, about our work with other people we have often been surprised that we have to reach back, past the media and education debates of recent years, in order to explain our approach. We find ourselves still charged by feelings and beliefs which have their source in our own training in the visual arts, so we had better sketch them in at the outset.

As art students in the mid-sixties we enjoyed the opportunities given by an economic boom, the rapid expansion of Higher Education, and a period of educational liberalism. We joined our contemporaries from working-class and lower middle-class families who were being given, for the first time, access to Higher Education. Our families relished the prospect of us moving up the social scale and we began to explore new and seemingly radical identities. By the late sixties, as we and other colleagues passed out of Art Colleges around the country, we carried with us – as we know did a much larger group – a strong but theoretically unclear conviction that a closer relationship between Art and society was necessary. We were intensely dissatisfied with Fine Art education and the contemporary institutions of art, which all relied upon and perpetuated a mystifying view of the creative imagination. We were angry about the blatant contradictions between a rhetoric of self-expression, the material privileges given to us in order to develop it at Art College, and the tenuous relationship it had to the world we were returning to. Above all, we shared a rejection of exclusive and élitist ideas about creativity being a special quality of gifted individuals, usually white men, which was not shaped by history, class and culture.

For many of us these views had been given initial shape by intellectuals who had found work in the newly, and contentiously, established Departments of Complementary Studies in the Art Colleges.[1] They had become a mandatory part of Art and Design studies which had been recently dignified by degree status. We found ourselves within institutions based upon the fiercely practical and intuitive traditions of late Romantic and modernist art while attending compulsory lectures given by refugees from the newer universities. The old linear, personality-based Art History began to be joined and challenged by the more contextual and analytical disciplines of literary criticism, sociology, social psychology, anthropology, and early film studies. With youthful seriousness some of us tried to make sense of this world we had entered, some of us were thrown out, others switched tracks and sought places in the universities themselves, still others were alienated by the potentially undermining effects of theory and withdrew into practice and subjective values. Those who stayed with it often grasped zealously at theory to test the taken-for-granted assumptions of a received practice and to penetrate the opaqueness of its institutions. As far as change was concerned, we naïvely overestimated the realism of this project. But a sense of the importance of theory as illuminating and generating (as well as being an outcome of reflecting on) cultural practice was a more lasting outcome of this encounter.

Practical outcomes

Some of our generation, who had been students in the radicalised Art Colleges of this period, subsequently went on to teach in them or other centres of Higher Education where art, historical, media, and cultural studies were getting off the ground. Others developed their own radical and 'critical' art practice and found, or so they believed, platforms for social intervention within the alternative, avant-garde galleries of the period. One outcome of these developments was the establishment of relevant courses and centres within Higher Education itself, rather than the formation of any newer, more popular, cultural and educational institutions. Even so, this limited and rather self-referring achievement can be seen as an advance, because the resulting redefinitions in theory did broaden the field of what could legitimately constitute culture and expression. This in turn changed what could be admitted as a study or activity in secondary schools, further and continuing education. It at least resulted in art and culture being talked and written about as cultural production; as something fully located in the social life of men and women.

The second outcome, a radical or even 'Marxist' art confined to new galleries and forums in old inaccessible warehouses, is harder to be positive about.[2] What was criticised was the incestuous cycle of Art, produced by Artists in Art Colleges, with an attendant art industry of gallery contracts, exhibitions and exports. What was 'struggled for' and put in its place was based on resurrected 'revolutionary' form *à la* Heartfield and others; symbolic references to social issues for leftish consumers of high art. But crucially, the work remained locked within art world circuits as if blind to its own social placement.

This then was our point of departure. A practical training in the visual arts extending to a practical and theoretical interest in contemporary media. A rejection, initially felt but increasingly intellectual, of the established and élitist forms which expressive practices took. An enthusiasm for social and cultural theory which at many points threatened to engulf us and become a substitute for practical expressive and educational work itself. But there were people, including the authors of this book, who took neither of the routes which we have indicated above.

Youth and class

The route that finally took us out of a period of working in Art Colleges and into the Cockpit Arts Workshop, included a lot of part-time work in schools, youth clubs and adventure playgrounds during the early 1970s. It was through these experiences that our own critical disaffection with available forms of cultural and educational work was given some positive direction. A fair number of ex-art students found their way into youth and community work at this time, as some still do although the area has become steadily professionalised and restricted. Many set about introducing photography, video, performance and mixed media work into the traditionally sport and craft based range of youth club activities. This could be a very difficult experience for the young youth worker. Often from working-class backgrounds themselves, they found their cherished skills and creative projects received only qualified acceptance, usually restricted to the mileage they offered for mucking about and taking the piss, from a new generation of working-class kids. Some persevered in this work, gradually moving away to set up, or join, the early community and youth arts projects.[3] Others, we know, grew away from their specialist concern with art practices and gradually became involved in general, pastoral youth work. For the community artists, creative and expressive work could remain central and young people who elected to, were expected to form up around its disciplines.

Youth and community arts projects established physical bases in working-class communities and arts workers learnt to develop open and informal ways of working. The scope of what was seen as appropriate to express through art was widened through these developments. But at the same time, the insistence of most community arts, workers and activists on working through the forms, styles and ideologies of contemporary high art, also led to a highly selective response from working-class communities. Surrealism, Dada, environmental constructions, art as play were the main things on offer. Photography was mainly documentary, realist, harsh, aestheticising the everyday environment. None of it was very popular although most kids would give it a try for an evening or two. Somewhere behind these practices was still the idea, the loose rationale, that they were somehow liberating, enriching; that they were, in the oblique manner of art, ways in which working-class youth might have their horizons broadened.

We still found this hard to accept, certainly community art practices were more accessible, democratic, and in touch with people's experience, but they were still fundamentally based upon the idea of individual creativity transcending the ordinary quality of everyday life through the traditionally prescribed 'mediums' of art. To keep art at the centre, as we have put it, and to expect the working-class kids that we met to see it as more interesting and exciting than their own cultural and symbolic forms, seemed untenable. Surely it should be the

other way round. The resources, skills, techniques, and conventions of representation and expression should be reworked, literally, in their interests. The question was how; what would this involve? Our early introduction to a sociology and politics of culture, whilst unable to tell us *what to do*, still held us back from a full endorsement of community art. In taking this position, cultural theory and analysis, as it was being developed at the Centre for Contemporary Cultural Studies at Birmingham,[4] was formative in the direction we took – especially the revaluation of popular culture and the idea of subordinate, generationally and class-based cultures as 'warrening' the dominant culture 'from within'. These ideas leave a lot out of account where creativity and aesthetics are concerned. However, as we discovered the absurdity and remoteness of traditional and avant-garde art practices from the point of view of working-class youngsters, we could begin to take seriously the vitality of their own cultural forms. We weren't left seeing our task as building bridges between our own radical versions of art or media practice and the worlds of young working-class people. We couldn't simply see our expressive practices as vehicles for their experience. We began instead a long apprenticeship to the worlds, values, and subcultures of youth; to their rituals, styles, and meanings – later written about by Dick Hebdidge in his book *Subculture: The Meaning of Style*.[5]

Mechanical reproduction

We have said that in the youth clubs, centres and projects of the early 1970s the initial reluctance of youth arts workers to loosen their grip on the forms and ideologies of art, had been positively offset by broadening its range of reference and demystifying it. Youth arts workers were also quick to recognise and take up the popularity of photography, video and simple mechanical print techniques in their work. Young people turned up for an evening session because a club or project was local, part of their territory or neighbourhood. Local people would often be in positions of control and influence, through formal membership of the management committee, related organisations like tenants associations, or perhaps even more powerfully, because they simply lived in the same street. They could all make their feelings about what went on known in very direct ways. Youth clubs often have quite long histories and are in touch with residual traditions of community solidarity, local politics and campaigns. There is often a sense of value for the voluntary sector and its support of independent education and recreation. Contemporary media production can be very social in nature. It has a clear need for audiences. Its potential for communication, celebration and documentation within communities made it an obvious winner for the young arts workers of the period.

Schools

Figuratively speaking, if you taught in a school, you could meet the same kids during the day that you met in the youth club in the evening, or in the holidays. But we encountered a much more depressing situation. Here we met, in a far more direct way, the watered down ideology of the Art Colleges in the school Art Departments. This was a crucial experience; it was our earlier experience as art students revisited but in grosser terms. The gap between what was claimed as being art in schools and the lived realities of many pupils was vast. It is probably this experience of being with working-class kids in the art rooms of inner city schools, and being alive to the irrelevance of what takes place to so many of them, that accounts for differences in our approach and that of photography and media teachers who are not so close to the institutional realities of art education. We can fully recognise the power of the claims made for art in education, as we recognise the value and enjoyment which it gives to our own and most middle-class and

a minority of working-class children, but we cannot deny or spuriously theorise away the active resistance of the majority. We soon came to see that for the majority of young people in the schools we worked in that Art was no less boring and irrelevant than any part of the academic curriculum. Resistance and disaffection was just as evident in these periods of licensed self-expression as they were in schools in general. It was, of course, anathema to say this. The currently rampant, popular and utilitarian ideology of the education reactionaries means that it is no less difficult, and certainly more dangerous, to say it now. But we were, and are, unable to respect the particular division of knowledge and practice which gave rise to a critical, socially and politically aware study of contemporary communication on the one hand, and a special preserve of pre-industrial modes of expression on the other. We could not and cannot accept that what is popular, current and experienced in our culture should be divorced from the timetabled spaces and resources for young people's expression in education.

Media studies

On this basis, our early projects at the Cockpit Arts Workshop aimed to bring young people to question and clarify their relationship to fine art and autographic representation, while suggesting the importance of mass and mechanical media. We ran mixed media projects within Art departments where through a sequenced programme of practical work, we hoped young people would come to understand something of the way in which photographs, TV, and print forms construct and mediate beliefs and values in society. We attempted to do this in ways which took up some of the immediate, topical and cultural interests of the groups we were given to work with. We made connections wherever we could with the social and political role that the autographic visual arts had played in pre-industrial society. We tried to recoup some of the active power of visual representation in history. In short, we offered young people in school, through practical work and discussion, a view of art as cultural production; we invited them to discover the historical and contemporary power of images in society. Again we made little headway within the subject itself, beyond the tangible enjoyment of working with some sympathetic teachers and young people who already knew a thing or two about the contemporary dimensions of images and ideology from experience. But we did generate a good deal of hostility even Inspectorial attention, from those who manage and safeguard the place of art in secondary education.[6]

This was occurring while, on a broader front, things were on the move in schools. It was quite likely that while we ran a project in the art room, across the corridor another teacher was watching, even making, a TV programme with a class. If they were making it, it would most likely deal with some aspect of contemporary life in a reflective and critical way. It might have taken the form of a simulated interview, an acting out of a relationship, perhaps a pastiche of a popular TV genre. If they were watching it, it would probably have been an off air recording of broadcast TV which they would discuss afterwards, or a specially made piece of educational TV which raised contemporary social issues.[7] These were the early days of Media Studies in schools, based as often as not in departments of English or Social Studies.

Progressivism

There was a larger context to these initiatives. The liberal comprehensive school of the 1970s was characterised by a high degree of local autonomy and related teacher-based, pupil-centred curriculum development. Progressivism was not a coherent movement and its course and pattern of achievement was uneven. Like the current Toryism, it was a response to and demand for change. A

demand for an overhaul of the educational system and a further opening up of possibilities for all groups in society. At a professional level there was a strong interest in examining the effects of the standard, established curriculum on the majority of pupils, a growing acknowledgement of the failure of the subject-based curriculum and a wish to loosen its boundaries. Correspondingly, there was an enthusiasm for developing, new areas of study which led to the encouragement of innovation and exploration of popular forms of educational practice. Within this there was an important strand of thinking which called for an extension of educational participation beyond the school to the community. There was a stress on the democratic management of the school, full participation of all teachers, and greater participation of pupils. Decision-making was to have the broadest possible base. Team teaching, integrated studies, block timetabling, school-based resources, and school-controlled syllabi were all outcomes of the progressive emphasis of the time. Within all this the Art subject seemed relatively untouched, it was separate, it sailed blithely on. For a long time, by concensus, aesthetic experience, and artistic or expressive practice were seen as transcending these politics of education. There were some exceptions but it took an official concern and centralised educational policy-making before cultural and educational dimensions of race, sex, and class made any impact upon school Art Departments. The Art subject was hardly ever part of the grass roots movement to which these policies were an official response.

Resistance

Despite our unhelpful location within the Art subject, we added our emphasis to the growing interest in media and curriculum development. Our particular stress was on practice, production, and process. We argued that if young people avidly consumed and valued, even if uncritically, the power of dominant media, that they should have the experience of producing their own messages, on their own terms and as part of their education. This was close to the view of some Media Studies' teachers who believed that practical work was a necessary part of coming to understand the ways in which the mass media construct meaning. For us it was also part of an aim to secure powerful and contemporary means of expression for young people in school. To the idea that young people might learn to decode dominant media messages by first encoding their own, we added two things. First, that they should, of right, be able to encode the meanings that they chose, that were significant to them rather than a Media Studies syllabus. Secondly, that this process should be taken seriously as expressive and educational work in its own right.

In the subsequent period there has been a parting of the ways between Media Studies and our own work in practical photography. In our view, some of the best and most democratic elements in the thinking that led to Media Studies work in schools, has been lost. As the area sought legitimacy, either by seeking a respectable place within subjects like English or as an examinable subject in its own right, it became academic. Clearly, there is a place for the systematic and discursive study of contemporary communications in schools, but this is not the same as the generally didactic and schematic approach which has come to characterise so much of the work in Media Studies.[8]

We noted above how we met resistance from within the Art subject to having its hallowed practice questioned. But more importantly, we also met resistance from the kids. It was from this that we learnt some important lessons. We saw this as resistance towards two aspects of the work we were then attempting. First, to our attempt to make young people's cultures the content of schoolwork, and secondly, a resistance to any challenge to their conceptions and views. We went on to believe that if you really want to engage young people in critical work, you

have to do this through the currencies and concerns of their own worlds. And then, if you want to base work on a valuing and exploring of young people's culture, you have to be in a position to offer them acceptable and powerful forms in which to do this. So, if painting and drawing, as expressive and representational means, don't spark off much enthusiasm, neither does reading texts which analyse the content of dominant communications seriously connect with their practical lives and perceptions. These were our conclusions five or six years ago. Since then we have been working on the possibility of a practice which can do both of these things. Essentially, this is the work that this book describes.

The period

We started this work one year before the Thatcher government was first elected, in the last miserable year of Callaghan's minority Labour government and the Lib/Lab pact. It was already a worsening situation for working-class young people and their teachers. Unemployment was rising generally and the figures showed that the young were being especially hit. Thatcherism emerged to dismantle and undermine the social institutions which provided for working-class people and the Trade Unions which defended them. The direct economic effect for young people has been mass unemployment; leaving school straight for the dole. The significance of this disruption in the transition from school to work has not been lost on Thatcherism. The anticipation of young people's resentment and unrest as their expectations are thwarted and squashed has been met by a number of practical and ideological measures. The need to provide some form of practical containment of working-class youth, as well as to 'restructure' the expectations they gain through school, has been met by an expanded and more powerful Manpower Services Commission.[9] The MSC has been the base from which to run the Youth Training Schemes and, independently of the Department of Education and Science, to effect a restructuring of the schools' curriculum. That the interests of Thatcherism lie in creating and containing a reserve army of cheap labour, rather than in extensive training to replace vanishing apprenticeships, is apparent in their recent attempts to make the YTS compulsory. Most working-class kids and their families have seen these schemes for what they are, the modern equivalent of the workhouse. The more complex and ideological role of the MSC has been to try to shift the expectations and attitudes of young people while they are still at school. In practice, this has involved shifts in how schools are organised and managed, and what they and the teachers who work in them do and perceive as their functions.

The liberal comprehensive school of the seventies was characterised by a high degree of local autonomy and related, teacher-based curriculum initiatives. This came under attack early on in the period of our project. It seemed as if the carpet was being pulled away just as we were finally getting started. With Callaghan's 1976 Ruskin College speech, a Labour government in office announced what was soon to become the new Tory agenda of educational accountability and standards. Having little to put in its place, Labour succumbed to pressure mounted from right-wing academics, amplified by a right-wing popular press. The accusations were of falling standards and rising indiscipline in the comprehensive schools. The comprehensive was deemed to have been established on shaky ground. The right claimed that all modern Social Studies projects and new methods of mixed ability teaching could not change the fact that children were born with widely different levels of intelligence; that it was wasteful and inappropriate, and the cause of all the problems in schools (and society) to give a liberal, critical, or academic education to those whose abilities suited them better to manual work or menial service.

This new Tory 'realism' has now established more than a foundation for the reintroduction of selective schooling in the public sector. A reformed educational élitism has once again replaced the liberal model of equality of opportunity. This sectional educational ideology has been interlocked with and reinforced by equally ideological claims that all services in the public sector are too expensive. The resulting wholesale cuts in public spending has been the other flank of attack on education. Behind the ideologies, the cost-effective rationalising, and the new vocationalism, lies the big stick of unemployment. In education the threat of unemployment is there to discipline teachers who may doubt the new wisdom, and to scare the pupils into accepting their daily dose of school work. The changes brought about by the politics of the last six years amount to a catalogue of worsening material and social conditions for teachers, youth workers, and young people alike. Many teachers have gone through amalgamations of their schools to find themselves working in a less responsive and democratic school structure. Enlarged schools, often on split sites, have more vertical chains of management justified as more efficient. New management tiers have been introduced to effect greater accountability, regulation of the syllabus, and monitoring of set standards. Teachers are more than ever encouraged to compete with one another to attain bureaucratic roles as the only effective way to attain a pay increase. A spurious order of specialism, merit, and classification now directs education and is being extended further and further downwards, to the point where inequality is enshrined as the natural foundation of the system. The last six years has seen the gradual, uneven but ceaseless erosion of the material and social gains of the last fifty.

The Cockpit

We have felt these changes in the state of education very tangibly through our relationships with hard pressed teachers and young people coping with, reacting to, or ingeniously avoiding harsh realities. But throughout the period our project continued. Its survival depended in part upon its being based in a specialist centre, the Cockpit Arts Workshop. This is not the place to write its history but it has been an important factor without which an account of the options and opportunities for work like ours would be seriously incomplete. We take a look at this in our conclusion and summary of future directions.

So far, in sketching the history of our approach, we have said little about young people themselves. They will, however, be at the centre of what follows. But there is a general point that we should make at the outset as it has informed the way we have related to and worked with young people.

The concrete and first-hand experience a teacher has of working with hundreds, perhaps thousands, of young people over a number of years, is constantly shadowed, even overshadowed, by society's dominant representation of youth. It can be hard to keep the two separate. Some teachers, as are many people generally, ready to allow this dominant view of youth to shape and colour their responses to the particular individuals and groups they meet. It is doubtful if any of us escapes this at times. 'Youth' is a powerful social category with strong connotations, and the capacity to signal moral panics. It confers a homogeneous identity on a whole generation. Real lives, real differences, even real similarities and affinities, can easily be lost sight of. At the very least our perception can be blunted and then open to assimilation to the stereotypes and myths about 'today's youth'. Many teachers and other people who work with youth try hard to avoid this. They test and challenge the dominant ideologies about youth in their relationships with them, and not the other way round. We hope that we can claim to be among their number. But, in the nature of ideology you can never, ever, be sure when it has crept up on you.

Work on family history and identity through photographs. From Yuk Man's project. (See pp. 117–22.)

The representation of youth

The mass-produced photographs which we carry in the following pages are adverts. Their primary function is to create markets. This is important and a fact that is hard to avoid whether you give them a casual glance in the street or subject them to semiological analysis in the seminar room. But our interest is at another level; it is in their presence. We point to them because they exist as the ideas and images of young people which a dominant culture circulates in close proximity to the routines and patterns of everyday life.

They are here to register the fact that on the vast hoardings which punctuate the streets we move in and in a wide range of popular and special interest magazines, we repeatedly encounter and consume ways of seeing young people. Together with the images and statements of film, video, television, and the popular press, these mass-produced photographs form part of a society's resources for representing a confusing and contradictory social world as a natural and sensible one. They are made by professionals with big budgets. They are paid for by wealthy and powerful minorities; the controllers of industry, commerce, finance and related institutions. It is by these means that young people are being continu-

BUILDING A SNOWMAI

Magazine advertisement, with insets, for Smirnoff Vodka, November

ally and publicly represented.

When brought together in one place, most selections of such representations beg to be ordered into a kind of composite biography or narrative.[10] Any one image implies a link with another. A story takes shape. A story of the vulnerable or innocent youngster, of futures to be planned, of romance and emergent sexuality, rebellion and waywardness, an accommodation to the realities of life and a settling down in material comfort. It is as if the paragraphs of a popular narrative had been separated and scattered around; pasted on walls, placed in shop windows and bus shelters; left lying on kitchen tables and stuffed between the cushions of a sofa. We piece the story together as we move about the city; between home and the street. The same basic story is told again and again but the details are always changing for the sake of topicality, credibility, and increasingly for tact.

In what looks like a concluding paragraph in such a narrative we see a young couple at home (pp. 10–11). Home looks like a terraced suburban house. Patio windows look out on to a strip of back garden. Alternatively, home could be a council flat of the kind built in recent years with its own small grassed area. There is this ambiguity in the image if you press it hard. It is an image which stays in touch with both aspirations and economic realities. It doesn't quite limit the possibility of having such a home to being able to raise a mortgage.

The style of the interior is fifties, Festival of Britain, with overtones of Hi-tech. Furniture redolent of the period of post-war reconstruction revived and used as part of a new ensemble of symbolic meaning. The room is bright and hard. It is contemporary in the sense of breaking with all that has become safe, stuffy, and complacent. It is not a nostalgic image but one where the style of a shrilly optimistic period, now alienated from the present, becomes a symbol for difference and modernity. The once popular artiness of the table lamp insults the soft exotic romanticism of the Japanese paper globes and Tiffany lamps of a parent generation. The style of the fifties underlines a generation's break with the weary, discredited cultures of the sixties and seventies. This looks like an ironic way of being in Thatcher's eighties.

'Smirnoff. Whatever you do with it its neat' – so runs the slogan. Neat also is the way in which this image of two young people in a room represents traditional and dominant cultural values clothed in a contemporary, almost subcultural style. Two categories of representation, two ways of viewing generation and lifestyle, the family and youth, are neatly and invisibly joined. Post punk, quasi rock-a-billy youth, streetwise code-breakers, spend a quiet evening at home – their home. Having a quiet (perhaps unpredictable) drink together. It's winter and warm inside. And cool. The nuclear family unit is reproduced with style. This could be the happy ending to the story of youth as it is dominantly told.

Nicki has a good job with a large company. She works at the head office on a word processor. Some good CSEs at school gained her a place on a diploma course at the local FE college. As part of the course she was sent to the company on a work experience placement. She decided then that she would like to work with them. She saw the girls in the bright, clean comfortable offices and the boss seemed really nice. You had to work hard mind you, and there was real trouble if you made mistakes or took too long about things, but there were lots of good things about it. You could wear smart clothes to work, the building looked out over the river and was air conditioned; it was like something out of a TV ad. You got luncheon vouchers and there were lots of nice snack bars and cafes in the area. The shops were good too and there was a health and leisure club nearby which she went to after work with some of the girls. You could also work flexi-hours which was handy. Anyway, she watched her manners while she was there and sort of smartened her image up a bit and they said they might have a job for her after college.

She's only getting £55 a week to start with but that's a lot better than some of her mates – those who've got jobs at all that is – the conditions are good and there are prospects of a secure future. Nicki is still living at home for the moment. She gives her Mum money for her keep and that leaves enough to buy clothes, go out during the week and pay her way, and still save a bit. Nicki likes a laugh and she's really into clothes. Her Mum reckons she's a bit of a devil and that £70 for an outfit that she'll wear only a few times is a waste of money – but you're only young once. Besides, she's got her head screwed on and she opened a bank account. She has her wages paid straight into it and is having a bit put into a special savings account each month. You wouldn't believe it to see her some-times – not exactly your typical investor! Still, she'd like a flat of her own soon. Perhaps on her own, or with a girlfriend. Perhaps even with Tony, the bloke she's being going out with, on and off, for a couple of years. He's keen but she's not sure yet if thats what she wants. There's a bit of the feminist about Nicki. She certainly doesn't want to

Cover of career pamphlet, November 1985

get stuck indoors all day with a load of screaming kids and piles of rotten ironing to do. But a flat with Tony would be nice; there's some really neat ones on an estate near where she lives with her Mum and Dad. Some of them have got bits of garden and you could make them really good. Nicki often wonders what it would be like, her and Tony in their own home perhaps staying in of an evening. One thing's for

LET YOURSELF GO

On the surface you may be the quiet type. Wouldn't say boo to a goose, all that kind of thing. But underneath there probably lurks a bit of a devil. And occasionally this other self needs to be let out for a bit of exercise. And when she steps out she likes to dress UP!

TAMI

Tami. Now who'd have thought that the girl lurking under the greatcoat would turn out to be so, er, *forward?* Tami went for The Big Impression in shirt (£28), waistcoat (£17) and trousers (£27.50), all from Lucy Clive at Hyper Hyper, 26-40 Kensington High Street, London W8. (Add £1 for postage and packing). The bra — which is *meant to* be showing — was £24 by Willy Brown at Old Town, 7 Upper James Street, London W1. This girl knows *no fear.* The socks (£1.25) are by Mary Quant, the shoes (£19.95) from Shelly's and the earrings (£8.99) from Miss Selfridge.

Feature illustration from popular teenage magazine, November 1985

Advertisement with graffitti, hoarding in Waterloo Station, London, October 1985

Illustrations from army careers pamphlet and National Westminster Bank brochure, November

certain she's certainly not going to become a typical housewife type!

Nicki's got two sisters older than her. One of them, Jackie is training to be a teacher. She's already got a degree.

She was always very bright and got a scholarship to Bishop Wilsons School which used to be one of those grammar schools, but now you have to pay to go there. Even the scholarship only went

part of the way to paying the fees and all the other things she needed. She went to France twice while she was there. But their Dad got a special loan from the bank, its especially designed for things *like schools fees or something and you can pay it off over a long time.*

Barbara, her other sister is training to be a nurse with the army. She's in Cyprus right now and is having a great time. She's always been keen on sport and there she gets to do a lot of swimming. She recently took up Scuba diving which she says is amazing. Jackie and Barbara are very similar really, they are both very sociable people, always doing something or other, and meeting up with friends. Reading Barbara's letters you sometimes wonder if she ever does any work! But you know she does and she loves it. She loves looking after children and has a really sympathetic way with people. She really would make a good Mum. No two ways about it. Actually, she is engaged to a bloke she met out there. He's doing an apprenticeship in some kind of engineering. Barbara says that when he's got his certificate he'll have a really responsible job and should get promotion quite quickly. People's lives will depend on his skill.

These then are the late paragraphs, the concluding images, in the dominant narrative of youth. Passages which tell you how traditional and adult social values are reproduced, or revealed, in a new generation. Even in a period of very high youth unemployment, they offer mythic and unlikely visions of fulfilling, even glamorous, futures in work and leisure. It cannot be accidental that the only really contemporary images of actual work situations, rather than training for work, that we could find at the time of writing depicted work in the armed services. These are images which address the concerns and responsibilities of a parental generation as well as youth themselves. They also reinforce and naturalise traditional gender roles in work and leisure. Young men are masters in their homes, managers or industrial technicians at work. Young women are happy in the office and the caring professions. Even the challenges of stereotyped ways of representing young women can be contained within older versions of the zany or wilful young woman.

In the narrative as a whole these images are preceded by those which represent youth itself. Youth as a social category; as a group seen as free from responsibilities and disciplines of the adult worlds. A group with its own distinctive culture; a problematic generation. It is in these images that we see youth gaining its undifferentiated identity – the youth of the 1980s and how they look, what they do. This is where a style and a look is pinned down and so made available for use in the more parentally oriented images which we have looked at, witness the rock-a-billy householder. For here the images, symbols and styles of youth are disconnected from the meanings which groups of young people have invested in them. Symbols of resistance and class or racially specific forms of expression become youthful, but conventional, activities and commodities. A way of dressing, a way of listening to music, a way of moving and dancing is taken from its location in the why and wherefore of young people and promoted as a characteristic of a generalised contemporary youth. Mean streets, dread sounds, sartorial styles which refute harsh realities, and cultish, even territorial display, can be orchestrated into an image of innocent, spontaneous leisure. Add an urban mural complete with simulated graffiti, foreground a Brixton Briefcase, 30watt RMS, LED meters pulsing, and a bureaucrat's Social Priority Area can become an Ad-mans Adventure Playground. (See pp. 18–19.) . The reality of young people is nowhere. Even the spectacular and rhetorical in their symbolic transformation of reality is appropriated by a dominant culture. It is used to lend authenticity to an image which strives to place youth as an innocent, ebullient group in an unproblematic social order. The dominant transforms the subordinate into the popular. Power trivialises and generalises what might otherwise threaten it. Serious things are happening in the images we pass by on the bus or flick through on the tube.

What then of the young lad whose environment will be improved by a tin of paint? and this youth with another ghetto blaster? (See p. 21.) He's less innocent somehow; jive walking the deserted streets against a dramatic evening sky. Is he the young man who later settled down with a Smirnoff? At this point he's easily linked to the strong implication of anti-social behaviour represented by the youngster with the spray can. The troubled youth who is the subject of a ludicrous piece of behavioural psychology. At times, it seems, this dominant culture is bold enough to admit and represent the existence of opposition and dissent. But again it does so at the expense of what is expressed by young people. In one case, moments of spine-tingling urgency and intimations of freedom carried by playing music on the move, through the streets, are reduced to caricature. In another, a youngster's anger and insight of the contradictions which surround him are pathologised.

There is obviously a blatent gap between this stereotypical tale and real complex lives of different young men and women. But it isn't the simple gap between reality and imagination, between truth and its image. The gap is between the world as experienced by young people and the way that world is dominantly represented. The fact that aspects of the way young

(Above and p. 19) Magazine advertisement from popular teenage magazine, November

people represent and express themselves in daily life are borrowed and used in these images complicates the issue. For young people do not necessarily contest these images of themselves. They may well accept the narrative as reasonable; as an attractive vision of the world they live in and of futures to enter. Like all images they address each viewer as an individual. They offer individual solutions to needs and desires which arise from the collective situation of young people, who are special victims of economic and social crisis.

Unlike the dry and instrumental ways through which the state seeks to impose ideas and shape the lives of young people, via increasingly repressive forms of education and training, these representations work through the currencies and meanings of everyday life. They deal with things that count: family, work, friendship, leisure, the major forms of life for young people. And, as is true of all media representations in our society, they are indivisible at many points from our experience of these forms of life. They are themselves forms through which young people, like all of us, come to imagine ourselves and others. But even as they strive, through the appropriation of young people's own images and symbols, to give credibility to their preferred view of society they can never close the circle of meaning, never absolutely ensure that we, or young people themselves, will accept their way of seeing youth. For even if young working-class people are drawn to accept some of the ways in which they are represented by the dominant culture, they also refute and subvert them.

This is shown most clearly in the way that, over a period of time, many working-class young people change their style, rework their identities and value systems as they experience and negotiate new struggles and options in their lives. As they adopt new forms of expression, create new images for themselves, often contradicting or ironically

commenting upon the real conditions of their lives, they repeatedly outstrip the current definitions and representations of the dominant culture. This may provide the generalising and incorporating dominant culture with endless opportunities for new commodity markets, but it also provides an arena of struggle over meanings and definitions between cultures. This is an arena in which working-class young people are as active and ingenious, if not so well resourced, as the professional representers of youth.

Dominant representations of youth cannot finally refute, and then define in their own interests, the experience of working-class young people. They cannot because they are unable to admit much about the real differences of life situation and viewpoint which are rooted in the experience of race, class and sex. Class can only be signalled by style. The social relations in which that style has meaning are left out. The specific realities of being female or black are similarly suppressed. These real social differences which determine how groups of young people experience the world and which set unequal limits on their futures would spoil the image, destroy the myth.

In the images which have formed our halting narrative, gutsy, up-front young women and cool, confident Afro–Caribbean youngsters have figured. But whether within the single image, or as part of the narrative which the selection implies, they are simply there as part of the paraphernalia of authenticity. They are not central characters in the script. Just keynote props. In obscure and tangential ways, which we have not set as our task to analyse in technical detail, they all lead to our final image. 'From Small Things Big Things Come' Vox Amplifier. Rock music, white working-class lad has become a rock star. The musical form most obdurately and repeatedly linked with youth and resistance, with oppression, is represented by the family man. Surrounded

Advertisement from colour supplement with (inset) advertisement from the popular music press, November 1985

by the signs of material wealth and substance, he plays with his small son.

Not bad for a rocker. Even better than a Smirnoff with the wife.

Photograph by Dave Hampshire

Advertisement from the popular music press, November 1985

Young people's style and popular identity

Early days

Mark Duke came to work on the Schools Photography Project in September 1979. He initially came as a member of a fifth year leavers' group who were timetabled to do photography with us as a 'work experience'[11] option.

This was the second year of our project to work closely with the meanings and modes of young people's informal expression. We

Photographic panel depicting 'two-tone' style, produced by Mark Duke and Peter as part of the Cockpit's Schools Photography Project, 1980

Mark Duke, photographer's assistant
Photograph by Dave Hampshire

had already discovered that the distinct youth styles of dress and music were a strong reference point in their early photographic work. With an earlier group we had developed the use of a Style Chart[12] as a way in which they could define and list current and distinct youth styles. They then plotted individually their relationships or affinities to them, using a scale of points. The Style Chart was used as the basis for photographic assignments to document the style of oneself and friends.

In that first term, Mark's own style was a mixture of soft Afro and Soul, a distinct but low profile style. By the summer of the next year his style had shifted considerably as he adopted the spectacular appearance of the

Rude Boy. Mark and his friends were involved in the working up of the 'two tone' style which became associated with the Anti-Nazi League and bands like AKA and Madness. Mark continued to work with us after he and the rest of his group had left school. He began to bring Peter along with him, a skinhead friend who was bunking off school at the time. Together they documented the 'two tone' style (see p. 23).

Mark also took pictures at home during the school project, using the 'weekend assignment' which asked him to photograph the style and lifestyle of family and friends (see (p. 25). These photos revealed the extensive interest, shared by his family, in style.

Mark became progressively more interested in photography. He began to work particularly with Dave Hampshire, the photographer-in-residence working from the Cockpit.[13] Shortly after he left school, Mark applied for a job as an assistant in a commercial photographer's studio and he came to us for references. He got the job. In that first year of work, Mark's style changed again as part of the Mod revival. Dave Hampshire photographed him as a Mod and at work. Mark and Dave became friends and remain so, and as he works near to our base Mark frequently calls in over lunch for a tea and a chat. Dave took another set of pictures of Mark at the beginning of 1985 (see pp. 26 and 27).

Mark's photographs, and photographs of Mark, span the period of the project which this account is based upon. Mark's work with us six years ago, helped us to establish and clarify an important relationship between photography and young people which we have developed in subsequent work. These early understandings came as a series of connections which are not normally seen together and acted on within education; connections between education and identity, representation, class, generation, and popular culture. For us they constituted both a dynamic way of approaching photography with young people, and a way of relating to their popular cultural experience. The key was and still is STYLE.

A selection of Mark Duke's early photographs taken on a 'weekend assignment', 1979

Photographs of Mark Duke taken between 1979 and the mid-1980s with Affro and 'two-tone' style, as a revivalist 'mod' and at work in a commercial photography studio

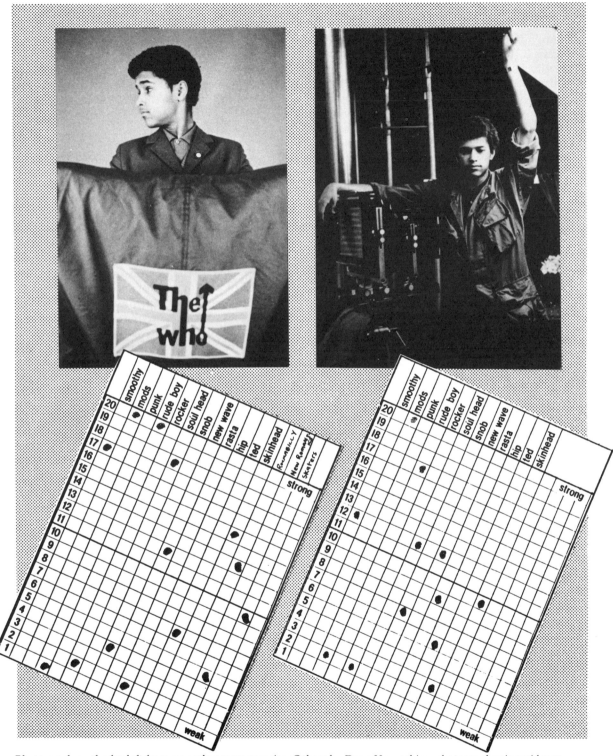

Photograph on the far left from an early group exercise. Others by Dave Hampshire, photographer in residence, working with Mark Duke

The popular

So many of the prevailing approaches within education, to photography, the media, and the cultures of young people, ignore or outrightly reject what is current and popular in them. In a very general way, we think this is so because to do otherwise would be to accede too much ground and potential power to the young themselves. The popular is widely perceived as a threat to the method and content of education. It is seen, by a whole spectrum of educators, and for different reasons, as trivial and no more than ideologically insidious. Simply, as the worst of a culture.

At best, education makes what is popular the object of critical attention: something to be picked over for what little meaning it contains. This exclusion or partial treatment of popular culture within the school syllabus is equally the case whether we look at photography, media, communications, or young people's interest in and value for music, clothes, and dancing. The negative treatment of all that is popular with young people points to an ideology within education; one that is professionalising and sectionalising and ultimately based on the class culture of people who control and maintain education. It is a view which ignores the place of generation and change as constitutive factors in culture and society. It also reinforces the unpopularity of school as an institution. There can be little chance of substantial and close educational exchange and growth if what is lived as informing and valuable by young people, is rejected as a starting point for educational work.

In rejecting the popular in photography an enormous closure is made in an area where a popular history and means of cultural expression are present but submerged. Mark and other students of these first two years more than demonstrated that photographic practice based on the snapshot[14] and their own lives could avoid any premature closure of interest or relationship. In fact it allowed us to avoid, in part at least, the most restrictive ideologies and practices of education and photography. It was possible to establish a practice which could take place in school time, as part of school work, and to which young people could relate through representing their current experience. So much school work fails to achieve points of relationship with what young people value and remains, instead, as something to be endured.

The discovery of an approach

The reason why many young people can have a strong and positive relationship to our projects is basically simple. First, photography is itself a popular practice with a currency in the family, and photographs are consumed as part of daily life as mass produced images. Secondly, photographs can depict what is valued in everyday life. The snapshot photograph of self and family form the main basis for an interest in photographic projects. The dynamic for its initial development is the changing positions of young people themselves. The key to the power which young people find in photography lies in its ability readily to provide images of themselves during a time, and through a period, of social transition. Although it can be variable in duration, all young people have to make the transition from being legal and social dependants within families to being wage labouring or propertied adults. It is through this transition and the specific form which it takes that a distinct sense of generation and social position is acquired. It is a time when identities are sought.

Interest in identity

The process of identification, of seeking to position yourself within or in a relationship to a culture, which young people enact as they go through transition, is complex and for the most part unknown. As adults, we have ideas and images of the process in retrospect as we talk of 'growing up', of being in one's youth, or of 'how it seemed then'. Also as adults, we sometimes make more formal representations of the process in the form of biographical reflections. But young people do in fact continually express their relationship to changing circumstances and to a range of possible or available identities. They do this mostly through the cultural practices they share with their peers. That is young people's self-identification since going through a transition is normally done together with others and in shared conditions. Within these conditions aspirations are tested out against the real and given options which exist for them as groups, as much as for individuals.

The imagined, glimpsed, or discovered future potentials of the peer group, as they are set by the material circumstances of the members' families and neighbourhoods, race and gender, are tested against the institutional possibilities and expectations available to them. So young people explore identities as so many ways of signifying the meaning they invest in membership of a cultural group. The actual signalling is done through a host of practices: manner of speech, physical posture, gesture, appearance, ways of relating or not relating to others, ways of ordering prioritising how time is spent, and attention to the context and location of these actions. Collectively these add up to the practice of style. A (life) style is then a considered and related set of signifying, culturally located practices.

The exploration of identity through its signifying practices has a special relationship to photography since photography is itself a signifying practice. A great deal of style can be carried by what is seen and what can be seen can be photographed.

The way young people see and use style in general, and the distinct, spectacular style of subcultural groups, is complex. The history and analysis of the emergence of youth styles, culture, and spectacular subcultures is also complex. Nevertheless, some understanding of both is necessary to the way we have approached photography with young people.

Not all young people have spectacular or even clearly defined styles; it is a minority who become the emissaries of style. Yet all young people have a relationship to the dynamic of styles at any given historical moment or 'slice' through a culture. Because style is as much about an imagined as it is an actual relationship to a culture, an identification with a style need not be visible. Style may be expressed through a choice of music or a discreet adaptation of more flamboyant articles of dress. Alternatively, it may be expressed only by a set of phrases or manner of address. Whilst most spectacular youth styles constitute distinct youth subcultures with autonomous customs and expressed beliefs, many elements of particular styles are softened and recombined by other young people at a clear distance. Here style is a mode of consumption; a way of discriminating in the market place – a matter which is not lost on the producers and suppliers of youth markets. Style, in this sense, is a stimulus to sales and a feature of the competition between manufacturers and suppliers. What appears to rise spontaneously from young people one day can be swiftly packaged and sold back to them the next. Equally, young people will include in their style items and commodities which are not directed at them and ignore those which are pushed under their noses.

Styles get imported, they are promoted through film and TV, yet whenever young-people have to claim a style as their own, rather than simply receive it, its acquisition is paced by the peer group. Its consumption is driven by the processes of identification within the transition from dependence to independent wage labourer or increasingly, what passes for such a status. So style as discriminating consumption gives all young people a relationship to it and their choices are made, in part, on the meaning encoded within the style.

The meaning of style

Where does the meaning of style come from and who makes it? If the answer was straightforwardly, the professional designers and promotors of commodities, then our argument about the importance of style to young working-class people would hold little interest. We would be simply saying that working-class youth have a consuming interest in what is provided for them; that they are good, if not avid, consumers. It would be foolish not to recognise that ex-art students turned entrepreneurs, designers, marketing agents and others, right through to buyers and shop assistants, play a part in shaping what young people wear or listen to at any one time. The same is true of the magazines they read, films and videos they watch, and which sports or leisure interests they rate.

The cultural interest in young people's patterns of consumption is extended once it is recognised that meanings, beyond obvious use and function, are coded in commodities and expressed through patterns of consumption. Conversely, these meanings derive from young people as much as they refer to them. The meanings of style are not hermetic precisely because the activity of young people is one of its sources. But because the meanings of style are also based in the (material) cultural practices of leisure consumption, they are inevitably routed through, and generalised by, dominant markets. For instance, American black youth of the industrial cultures of Chicago, New York and Los Angeles have had many of their style-based expressions of resistance exported through complex market chains to London and from here to other parts of the country.

In London, in 1985, the youth leisure markets became so specialised that it was possible to track through, in quite precise ways, the youth styles which had accrued since the 1950s. The classic styles of the Teds, the Mods, Rockers, and Skinheads are all available as modes of dress from specialist suppliers. Rasta, Rudeboy, and Rockabilly music can be tracked down to dusty, almost Dickensian shops around Soho, and small stalls tucked away in inner-city markets. The styles and subcultures now have well-documented histories in expensive large format paperbacks. Much of this specialist marketing represents the presence of a small minority of youth whose interests are more in reliving moments of authentic style than

they are in mass revivals. For the styles have moved on and have been reworked, and while no less spectacular, they are more outwardly conforming to the dominant parental culture.

The depressed capitalist economy of the eighties creates a singularly contrasted context to the short post-war boom in which the very first working-class youth styles emerged. And the current styles on the streets seem to have little obvious or overt sense of resistance to a society which is making youth bear the brunt of the crisis of profitability. The current smooth styles play subtly and ironically with images and signifiers of wealth and quality. Young people who may not have a bus fare between them will promenade, displaying what looks like gold worth investing, soft Italian leather shoes and jackets – contrived display of wealth in a context of unemployment and poverty.

Decoding the meaning of style

There is no readily available method and no clearly resolved theory for decoding style practices. There are some theoretical signposts and axioms which can be brought to bear upon the particular quest to understand the cultural practices of a specific group of young people, or the relationship of young people to a worked up and defined style. But it seems to us that each new enquiry will have to break new ground, for if style practices are explorations of unconfirmed cultural identity then there is a historical dynamic at work propelling youth, theorist, and teacher alike into unknown realities. The basic building blocks in the cultural analysis of style must come from a sense of historical dynamic. One that is based upon and paced by class society and its conflicts, contradictions and antagonisms.

Analysts who looked at the Mods with a historical materialist perspective saw at the centre of spectacular youth subculture attempts to resolve, on a generational basis, the larger conflicts and contradictions of the post-war, English working class. Subculture

Some representations of photography as young people meet them

was seen as a magical, mythical, or symbolic attempt to retrieve social cohesion in the face of the actual break up of working-class communities.[15] In an even broader view, subculture was seen as the space in which young working-class people resist and subvert their subordination to the dominant logics of the labour market. Similar lines of analysis, into forms of symbolic resistance to domination, have explored the oppression of Afro-Caribbean youth in a racist and colonising culture and the oppression of young women in a patriarchal culture. So the lines of analysis are now exceptionally complex and much of it remains theoretically innaccessible. But what is clear is that style practices are a significant means for young working-class people to explore cultural affinities and identities. And that this arises through the continual discovery by young people of the contradictions within a society and a culture structured by inequality and exploitation. The question has long been how to do more than write about it.

Some representations of photography as young people meet them

Photography as a Cultural Practice

Developing a photo practice

How to take pictures

We are aware that for many teachers the first question about how to take pictures is: what to take pictures with? The answer to this might mean anything from the politics of persuading an HOD or Head to create a budget for equipment, persuading another department or MRO to loan equipment, trying to get a broom-cupboard darkroom appr-oved by health and safety, through to more detailed questions about what equipment to use and what materials to buy. In short, one of the main obstacles to practical photography is its reliance on relatively ex-pensive plant and a more

Pupils in a classroom, South London comprehensive
Photograph by Cockpit Department of Cultural Studies

than average per student running cost. The prehistory of most photographic projects will be the description of the arguments and tactics for acquiring the material basis for any photography to occur. Whilst we don't intend to go into this in detail here, it is clear that part of any strategy for establishing photography as a viable option in a school,[1] youth or community centre, will in part involve justifications for its legitimate inclusion and, much more, the pragmatic process of arguing for monies from the institution's budget. In the absence of any empirical research to support us, it nevertheless seems likely that, looked at over a number of years, photography could prove viable within a school's economy if compared to other technical practices. Also, within an education authority, there would be much scope for equipment loan, shared equipment and access to more specialist resources. In our own work in schools, we have functioned on the material basis of a maximum of four 35mm SLR cameras for maximum group sizes of twenty, with access to either an onsite school darkroom (average of two enlargers) or an offsite large teaching darkroom (four enlargers) or both. Materials' budget for projects, run on an average half a day per week for three terms, are between £60 and £100, depending on the kind of work involved and the form of production employed.

Assuming access to the minimum of equipment necessary and a reasonable budget for film and paper, we can consider the question: how to take pictures? The single most important organising principle in considering how to introduce photography is that of establishing a practice. This means that from the outset the larger purposes and intentions of any project are spoken through the practice and that it is through the practice that we address all questions of meaning. Although this may seem obvious we cannot stress its importance enough. The practice must be understood as the point of relationship between ourselves and the students. The significance

of this principle is based in the recognition that photography is a developed and available practice to the students as it exists in popular culture and as they will undoubtedly understand it. The more abstract point behind this, as we outlined in the introduction, is that it allows everyone to make images which are not dependent in the first instance on a learnt skill or developed intention. Understood this way there is something in the assertion that taking photographs has an equivalence to Michelangelo painting the Sistine ceiling or Dickens writing *Hard Times*. The point being that the currency of the photographic image is based in its mechanical reproducibility. Anything less than building a photographic practice from the outset runs the risk of reducing the social status of photography. To use photography as an adjunct to the existing forms of school work, or to subordinate it as a school subject, reduces its possibilities and photography merely becomes a technical aid, a resource, a branch of physics. Although these specific uses of photography have real value, they are not the same thing as the practice of photography. Of course, there are still ways of starting to do photography, from laboured technical instruction and abstract rehearsals about what is involved to what the project is about.

We need next to outline what our method involves. The key to organising the taking of pictures from the position we've just outlined is in the recognition that photography does have a popular currency and use. So whether the students have taken photos before or not, or whether they've used Instamatics or SLRs, they will all have understandings about what photographs are, what photographs typically show. It is important to work with this body of popular knowledge, to accept the prevailing assumptions about the nature of the photographic image and its uses; in effect, to establish photography as it is met and practised by young people outside school and largely within the family. The basis of this practice will be the snapshot where the camera is regarded as a fixed mechanism for recording what is within the field of view of the lens. The image that results from this is then seen to correspond directly to a moment in time, of the events, objects and places in the external world. The snapshot then contains a view of an external verifiable and varying reality – it is the window on the world. Seeing photographs this way, all cameras are Instamatics, even though they are manifestly not and we may be aware that the photographic image is a constructed and mediated version of reality. The point is that you can, and the majority of people *do*, use cameras on the basis of the snapshot.

In using 35mm SLR cameras to take first pictures and recognising the need to take pictures from the outset, it is possible to reduce the technical instruction on their use by presetting the shutter speed for given lighting conditions, leaving only focusing and metering to be mastered. Even this can be done as you explain it to a group by passing round the loaded camera, trying in turn to focus, meter and click. The explanation of focusing is virtually self-evident (you'll get a blurred or fuzzy picture if the image in the viewfinder is not sharp) and metering can be reduced to 'if you don't get the needle in the circle (or between the + or −) your picture will be too dark or too light'. Additionally, if a film is being used in this explanation then the contact sheet used on the following session will be evident proof of results. So generally we're saying, keep explanations to a minimum, start to take pictures immediately, don't challenge the popular status of the image, organise the use of cameras on a shared group basis.

What to take pictures of?

The answer to this depends very much on the conditions of time and space in which you're working. Assuming that much of this introductory work will be done in school, in the classroom and in the timetabled period, or the equivalent in youth club terms, the likelihood is that there will be four walls of which one will be windows, a room full of desks and chairs, you, and a given number of young people. In this situation, and given the possible 360 degrees in which you can point the camera, the most obvious subjects are the people in the room.

In passing, we must add that there is no necessity, as far as instruction on camera use is concerned, to stay in the classroom, since within any given time it is possible to move somewhere else; another part of the school, activity centres in the school, the immediate surroundings of the school, or even down to the local shopping centre. Instruction of the kind we think is necessary can and has been given on the top deck of a bus. But in any eventuality wherever you go, taking pictures of each other will, for the student, be a priority subject and unless you've got a very passive student group probably impossible to stop. This in itself is as good a reason as any to move out of the classroom. Photographing friends is a legitimate, popular subject and snapshots of oneself are a continual source of interest. For young people this is even more so, as looking at oneself, whether in the shop window reflection or the mirror in the cloakroom, is an important way of checking your image, your social identity.

Giving shape to this interest

A whole series of introductory exercises can be built up around the given interest in self-image, whatever subsequent work you undertake. In the majority of our own work it has become a greater and greater interest, and increasingly complex in character. The work of these early exercises is

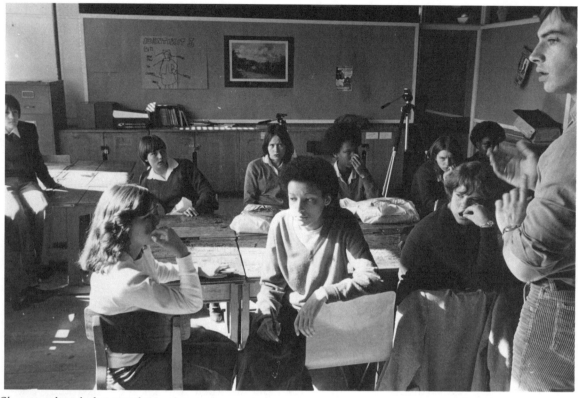

Classroom-based photography session
Photograph by Cockpit Department of Cultural Studies

partly to build up a confident and independent use of the camera, important for later work where results matter more or the possibility of retakes harder to achieve, and partly to progress to more complicated aspects – the stress on framing, distance and angle being the most obvious – and also to realise the symbolic power of the photographic representation of self-portraits. In practice, all these stresses are present as different ways of photographing each other are established.

Some introductory exercises

Mugshots

The possibilities for humour are always present in photographing a friend. This humour is realisable both through the photographer's control of the camera and the photographic subject's response to the camera. Again, without structuring, these possibilities are recognised and acted upon by students. It is only one step to structure the possibility very early on in

an exercise. The mugshot exercise employs captions and props to hand, plus the conscious use of gesture and posture. It is really a game based on the public figure, whether presented on a newspaper front page, magazine, poster or record sleeve. It is also a recognition that the photograph is a tranformation of a private to a public image, and that the photograph is a necessary part of being publicly known, of the process of becoming a celebrity. Part of the game relies on very simply phantasy projections which go from credible, real and held aspiration to the ridiculous and comic.

Self and context

This is an exercise in which you ask students to photograph themselves with or against objects, places and people with whom they identify and it needs to be carried out in a known location outside school. The local shopping parade or high street is, in our experience, one often chosen by students and usually within easy striking distance. This exercise also has further technical sophistications which might include asking students to take each particular location three times, varying the angle or distance in each case. Either way it is important to sort out groups, perhaps working in pairs, and leave them to do it, arranging to meet them at a certain place in an hour's time, or saying you will stay in a certain place so they can return if they have any difficulties. The strength of interest in this exercise usually lies in the authority or credibility of the resulting photographic image. If, for instance, you photograph yourself lean-

'Mugshots'. Early image and caption exercises

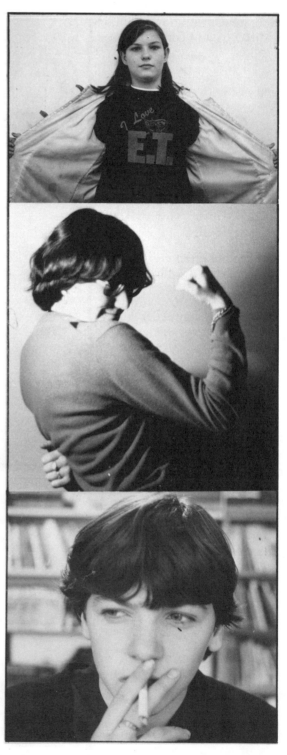

Extending the 'mugshot'. Photos taken by pupils of one another, having a laugh and presenting an 'image'. Use of props, gesture, expression and stance

Taking snaps of one another in the classroom (see page 35)

ing on an expensive car, then the implication is that you own it. If you are photographed entering an expensive shop or a bank, it is assumed that you have some business there. For the students this has endless possibilities; going in, coming out of pubs, sex shops, banks (typically boys), showing oneself as a worker, in the office, at the typewriter, hairdressing. Or, more naturalistically, photographing each other in places of interest – the coffee bar, McDonalds, a record shop. The other possibility rarely to be missed, is that of having a laugh, basically photograp-

Early snaps from a 'self and context' exercise in the school's locality

hing yourself, or each other, doing prohibited things, using objects and facilities for purposes other than they are intended for, drawing attention to yourself, faking, posing; endless invention, mocking adult roles and identities, or, as in the former examples, aspiring to adult identities or acknowledging a specific youth practice. In discussing these photographs later and in providing a criteria for selection and printing, clues can be found as to the basis of individual interest and identity which become important in orientating further work. It is not hard to see that there are variable versions of this exercise along a formal – informal axiom of controls and demands. What interests us is the degree to which basing photographs on self and friends is sustainable over long periods of time.

Rockabilly style. An early photograph from an extended project at the Cockpit by Arts Council Photographer in Residence Dave Hampshire

A first look at styles

Still holding on to the idea of photographing each other, this is the obverse of the image and context exercise. You ask the student first to take full-length shots of each other and then take details of clothing, jewellery, footwear or hairstyles which they think are special to the person in question. The results are rather like poor fashion photos or mail order catalogue pictures. What is important, however, is the inventory of symbolic objects which results, a recognition, however small, that there are two orders of representation, that the hairstyle itself is a representation of meaning and that the photograph of the hairstyle is a further representation of that meaning. Quite a complex process is at work here in a relatively straightforward exercise. Working in pairs or small groups, students are using the camera to 'read' each other in terms of the symbolic meaning inscribed in various material aspects of dress, hairstyle, make-up, jewellery, posture and expression. Of course, they 'read' each other anyway, the signification through material objects being like a language. In the normal course of events, the meaning goes uncommented upon, although there will be a lot of discussion of how symbolic effects are

Examples of a developing awareness of framing and use of signifiers within early 'self and context' work

(Above and p. 44) 'Working in pairs or small groups, students use the camera to "read" each other in terms of the symbolic meanings inscribed in various material aspects of style'

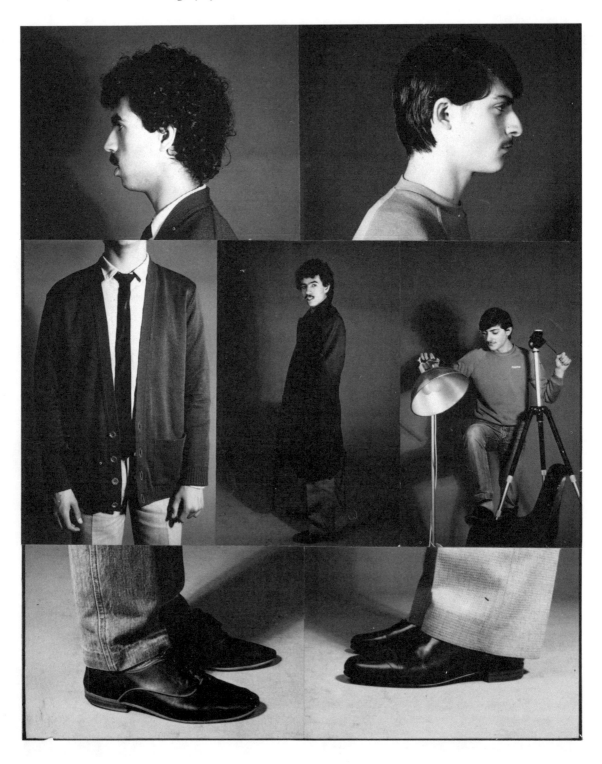

A first look at style: using a simple studio set-up. See page 41

A discussion between a group of 5th-year students before embarking on an assignment

achieved. Since this signification is based on material objects, a lot of discussion will inevitably centre on where things can be purchased and for how much. The importance of the photographic 'reading' of style is precisely that it re-presents what is already a representation and that it can do this better or worse, sympathetically or otherwise. In short, it draws attention to the constructiveness of photographic and symbolic representation. It also and equally, importantly, has an expressive dimension which has less to do with understanding photographic conventions and much more to do with using conventions to produce desired or self-affirming self-portraits. The camera no longer renders the individual as in the snapshot – the mugshot 'realism' mode – but as a contrived, most likely glamorous figure.[2]

Early printing – What to print?

The general argument we used to suggest that the initial organisation of photography should centre on taking pictures can also be applied to printing. The insistence is on building a substantive practice and

A selection of prints from another early exercise in which students scan an area for signs, symbols and objects which have interest and meaning for them

(Above and p. 48) 'Classic' snapshots of friends and people at work and animals, younger brothers and sisters in early selections of 'what to print'

that must obviously include all the stages in the production of pictures. Being able to make an enlargement of a negative taken the previous week opens up the process of selection and control, and consequently begins to erode the naturalised view of the photograph as instantaneous and automatic, in effect the practice has the potential to demystify the medium. This understanding was raised to a general principle in the many community darkrooms and photographic projects which developed in the early 1970s and is an important emphasis on access to and control over the medium. In itself, though, it is insufficient in enabling young people to establish a practice primarily because in increasing access to a general principle of teaching it marginalised questions of meaning, in effect it prises off technical considerations from the meaning and use of pictures. The approach we adopt emphasises practice but attempts to hold together the technical and evaluative. As with taking pictures, this again means being sensitive to and working with commonsense views of photography whilst working eventually for a practice based on the

Apart from the self, other children and local workers are favourite subjects for early prints

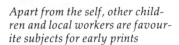

'Photography is a rather gendered practice'

conscious use of photographs, as constructed at every point in its manufacture. The most available and easily understood point at which the technical and evaluative are held together is in selecting which frame on a contact sheet to print. Looking at contact sheets and defining the criteria for selection has then to be established as a practice. Most of the common-sense views of photography militate against this particular stage, since the image at the

One afternoon around the Elephant and Castle; from doing a little boy a favour to more work on self-image

point of taking the picture is largely understood as automatic and representing a real moment in time. The consequences of this is followed through to a technical process of transfer from negative to positive. In our experience this leads the students to rush through the process in order to get a result, to get a tangible print. Given the way pictures are produced commercially this is reasonable, photographs are commonsense objects, produced to be consumed.

Obtaining a result is obviously important and we, as much as the students, are interested in their subsequent use and value as a commodity which can be put on display, or in an album, given to a friend or relative, or simply carried around in a pocket or bag to be eventually lost or thrown away. In order to meet this demand it is possible to simplify the printing process. A set of standard procedures can be worked out which, in similar vein to our teaching about how the camera works, presets the enlarger aperture, keeping light constant and leaving only the length of time to determine the correct exposure. Test strips can be precut and a standard of two-second intervals over eight divisions will nearly always give a range including the correct exposure. Developing, stop and fixing times can be displayed next to the trays, focusing on the enlarger is self-evident. The simplified method should be a foolproof guarantee of an acceptable result although in the initial haste to get the print, students often attempt to find a fixed exposure time for every negative, don't fix the print for long enough or don't wash the print for long enough. The acceptable result has wide latitudes. What is clear is that in the majority of cases it is *social rather than the technical criteria* which dominates the process. Students will not, unless instructed, select the best exposed negative to print but the image they have most immediate interest in.

Making selection a part of the practice

It is the interest students have in getting results and in the manifest content or meaning of first pictures which form the basis for establishing a practice concerning selection, but with the recognition that common-sense views will work against lengthy discussions. The practice of selection must take into account the recognised need for results. The following exercises were designed to provide a criterion for selecting which pictures to print from introductory exercises and from first out-of-school assignments. They nearly all rest on an axiom of best to worst, or an order of shots according to given criteria. The importance of this way of structuring is that the criteria can be both varied – you can treat the same contact sheet according to differently given criteria, and centred on the students own value and discrimination. Also, it is directly practical and purposeful simply to decide which pictures to print.

Best or worst of self

From the introductory exercises of mugshots, image and context, in fact all the pictures the students took of each other, there is always a strong desire to have enlargements of pictures of yourself or friends. It is often the occasion for incriminations against the photographer for taking bad or technically ruined shots, or an occassion for making the claim that there isn't a 'good' picture of oneself. It is also the occasion for humour, usually at others' expense at a particularly unintentional silly expression or a deliberately set-up humorous snap. If the criteria for selection were not specified then obviously much of the above would be in play; in providing a best–worst axiom you are simply ordering what is already being act-

Selection of prints on the basis of use value (left column), and interest value (right column). See page 53

ively worked on. In the following example it worked like this. The students were asked to select the best picture and the worst picture they took of someone else. We did not discuss at this point what we meant by best and worst. They did this outside the darkroom, working together and marking with chinagraph or felt tip the selected frames on a contact sheet before printing them. We then used their selection as the basis for discussing with individuals and the whole group why they had chosen the frames they did. This we must add, as an early discussion, was not very full and there was both a great deal of reserve on their part in talking about pictures of themselves and friends and also a limit in language as to how to talk about them. Nevertheless, some things were clearly established. The common criteria for best–worst of someone else was technical, mostly focusing and exposure, rather than framing and angle, and the criteria for best–worst of self that of subjective flattery.

Use value – interest value

We went on to use another contrasting criterion for the same group's first out-of-school pictures where we asked them to select, initially one for each category, on the basis of interest and use. Again we did not spend any time explaining what we meant by this, leaving it instead as self-evident. The results show how it is understood and relates to the social currency of the print. Use value seems to correspond entirely with the snapshot conventions; a picture of a friend for a friend, a member of the family for the family. Interest value worked as a criterion for defining the subject – interest in subjects like animals, or interest in the photographic print, which would be a technical interest. At this introductory level defining a criterion for printing is important, especially where a specified use for the pictures has yet to be given. Later

when students are working within forms of production the criterion comes increasingly from the demands of the form. But here the criterion establishes useful habits of looking at contact sheets carefully, of distinguishing between several similar pictures, and, most importantly of all, talking about the meanings, intended or otherwise, of the shot taken. The best–worst axiom can gradually give way to more sophisticated criteria, where, for example, you ask students to select, from the weekend assignment, six or more from thirty-six frames which are most representative of their own or families' lifestyles. This clearly begins to involve narratives, contrasts and comparisons, juxtapositions between pictures. Effectively a practice is being built up.

Making the lived present

First of out-of-school assignment

One of the recurring problems for English or Social Studies teachers wanting to include material on contemporary culture in their programmes of work is that of the availability of resources. Albeit that in the sphere of public representations 'texts' for study are bountiful – TV programmes, newspapers, magazines, advertising and consumer products. Beyond these forms the discrete 'text' evaporates. What, for instance, would be the 'text' for the experience of the football match, of being with your mates, brothers and sisters on the terraces of your team's home ground? Or what would be the 'text' for a Friday night 'blues', a sound system competition at the local youth club, having 'a larff' around the flats, working on a stall on Saturday morning, working at Woolworths, Boots, or the local bread shop? Of course, all these could be classified as elements of a number of themes in Social Studies, 'Work and Leisure', for

Selection of prints from a 'weekend assignment'. See page 57, 'Wording the assignment'

instance. They could be discussed, questions asked, comparisons made with other social groups and essays set, no doubt – we've seen such syllabi. But this is not what is being posed here, which is how does the everyday life of our students become an object of study – and what sort of 'study'? What are the forms by which it is communicated to themselves, how do they represent it to themselves? Most obviously (and here is where most school work at all concerned with the valuation of everyday life centres itself), it is continuously spoken. But for this to become a 'text' it has to be 'stilled', held in some form or other, its continuousness has to be interrupted. A great deal of skilled English teaching has concerned itself with the translation of continuous speech into the written text – the poem, autobiography, fiction. Drama teaching has also developed techniques for representing, re-encoding the continuous spoken form; improvisation, role-play, simulation and performance. In the cases of English and Drama, texts are being constructed out of the experience of everyday life; texts which embody the beliefs, conceptions and feelings of the participants; texts, which in the best examples of such work, are put into circulation – as in the work of Centreprise,[3] or workshop theatre groups. They become expressions, representative forms with real currency for particular groups. In a much narrower sense they also become school work, since all school work is concerned with the production of texts for circulation – typically, though, a form of circulation between individual students and individual teachers, texts to be marked, assessed, evaluated, compared. In both senses, however, we can acknowledge the point that 'texts' are being constructed, experience is being encoded in a communicative form, representations of the world are being made. This must be regarded as a base line in the understanding of school work as a cultural study, a first step from which a multitude of practical and theoretical teaching problems stem, which

continually and recurrently surround the meaning of such expressions, their status and use as understood by students in school and in relation to the wider culture. Staying on this base line for a moment, we can understand photography and the production of the photograph in a similar fashion. The photograph is also a text which can be studied, and established work in media studies has developed quite formal ways of analysing the photographic text as it appears in a range of public representations. It would be hard to ignore the importance of the photograph when examining the popular press, advertising, a range of magazines for targeted social groups, etc. Indeed the photograph often occupies a dominant role in such publications and it becomes hard to separate the photograph from the print which is either directly on, or combined with, the photo, as in much advertising, or accompanying the photograph as a caption, a headline, or extended factual/fiction written account. Such work as this is that of decoding the text, taking apart the messages, cracking the code by which such public representations are made (a good example here is Judith Williamson's *Decoding Advertisements*.[4] But what, as we started out by asking, are the photographic representations when we move beyond public or dominant representations to everyday life? The most developed historical form for the photographic representation of everyday life is that of the family album which is a rich and underdeveloped source of popular history, although there are real problems in acquiring access to them and of making what is largely understood as a 'private' text a resource for use by a student group. There is a further problem which we touched upon in the earlier discussion of the structure and content of the family album, which is that the family album is partentally centred, and while massively overlapping with the culture and practice of students (since we live in families) is not necessarily inclusive of their experience. Beyond the family album there is very little at

Contact sheet and one selected enlargement from a 'weekend assignment'

a popular level, although the work of Jo Spence in *Beyond the Family Album* is suggestive of ways in which the form can be extended as a continuing record of individuals. To go beyond the family album is clearly to move beyond the received cultural text and the work of decoding it, to encoding work. To see the photograph as the English or Drama teacher might see work on written or dramatic form, as the process whereby experience is being encoded in a communicative form, representations of the world are being made. And it is here, as the English or Drama teacher meets it, that our multitude of practical, pedagogic, organisational and theoretical problems arise, and it is time that we move off the base line to look more closely at what is involved in the particular representational form of the photograph.

We have already spoken about the organisation and introduction to practical photography in the timetabled period; how with limited equipment we can nevertheless start building a rudimentary photographic practice, where technique and content are held together through a series of introductory exercises. We've seen how even within these limits, under restrictive conditions, students can and do take up a practice in relationship to their continuous lived stances, beliefs and outlooks. This, as we've discussed, is done by (a) making the student the obvious subject of first pictures, and (b) by structuring the brief to include recognitions of the constructedness of the image, simple manipulation of meaning – shifts of foreground– background relationship, shifts in contexts, connotative objects, captions, etc, as well as importantly accepting their existing use of the snapshot. It would be hard to claim much for these first images which are spontaneous and undifferentiated – immediate responses to using the camera, although in the ways we've discussed they are not simply put aside as a means of technical facilitation, but in the subsequent work of looking at a contact sheet and decid-

ing which negatives to enlarge we are encouraging selection on the basis of their interest and use.

Through the introductory exercises we can monitor individual problems with the use of the camera, iron out technical difficulties to the point where the students feel reasonably confident about using a 35mm camera flash and independently. The first out-of-school assignment marks a qualitative change in the practice, more than anything because the students are entrusted to carry out a piece of work on their own. Teachers have often queried the advisability of lending expensive school equipment to be used unsupervised, and it is something that students recognise as a problem as well. They may well trust themselves to look after the camera, but are often worried about their responsibility if the camera is lost or stolen. Some students have refused for some time to take a camera home for precisely this reason. Yet in the three years we have been lending cameras, regularly and, throughout the school year, we've only had one camera stolen, and that was on school premises by an intruder.

There is very little alternative but to accept this risk if the photo-practice is to centre substantially on students' practical lives. There is, after all, a limit to what you can take pictures of in schools or during school time.

Wording the assignment

Our most developed experience of out-of-school assignments has been that of the weekend project (mentioned earlier in first exercises and discussed more extensively further on), which has now been carried out by well over a hundred students. Very simply, it involves lending a camera to students over the weekend and asking them to take a number of pictures. The complex part is what you ask them to take pictures of, how in the wording of the assignment

Contact sheet and one selected enlargement from a 'weekend assignment'

you make it clear that you want them to be highly selective and discriminating about showing things which they consider significant, without you knowing in any one case what that interest will consist of, and without wishing to 'determine' the outcome by specifying the subject. It might be suggested here that we are making too much of this and that in centring the content of the practice on what the students think is important, we should simply leave it to them. In effect, to word the assignment to say – take pictures of things that interest you. This, of course, can be done, but it should not be imagined that this will produce 'authentic'

results, or results which directly correspond to students' interests. Our view is that there will be qualitatively different results from different instructions, apart from the fact that instructions are often deliberately subverted, which we discuss elsewhere. If you say, 'take pictures of anything' – i.e. leave it totally open for the students to define – the results will show a range of culturally prescribed subjects and conventions of representation.

Apart from the common subject matter of friends and family, girls take pictures of babies, animals and flowers, and boys take pictures of cars, motorbikes and girls.[5] It needn't be

quite so stereotyped as that, but it is the case that saying 'take anything' in the wording of an assignment means something quite specific in photographic terms. As we commented earlier, this recognition does not rule such an assignment out, and of course, the culturally prescribed subject is present in virtually all pictures. Cars, cats, babies, bikes, apart from being real, are carriers of symbolic meaning and to represent them photographically may well be to signal this symbolic value for a variety of reasons, desires and aspirations. At the same time, these reasons will all be equally culturally prescribed. In the examples we're considering here the

cultural prescription of interesting photographs is clearly based upon gender identities – girls like babies because they will as adults produce and care for them, boys like bikes because they will as adults aspire to or actually own one, that motorbikes are inscribed with meanings of power, etc.[6] It is, in our view, possible to be more refined than the 'take pictures of anything' as a first out-of-school assignment. In the weekend project we gave students the following written instructions: 'Take pictures of the style and lifestyle of your family and friends (remember this can include objects as well). Use all your film.'

We rarely explained this instruction further nor have we been asked to by students. It has been taken as a self-evident and reasonable thing to go and do. Whilst it is still a very general instruction it is clearly less than everything and anything. It states who to photograph and implies something about what aspect of these people to represent and it gives the photographer an orientation in taking pictures. At the same time, it doesn't specify individuals and locations neither does it specify what 'style' is, and finally it does not specify which way to photograph them. From our point of view, it is a safe bet that for any student their significant social world will be made up somewhere between family and friends, and that the concept of style is a recognised way of referring to what is pertinent, valued and particular to individuals and groups as lived practices. The general point to make here is that we are not trying to pose the method whereby ideological or mythic interests can be superseded by authentic and real interests in what is represented photographically. What we are posing is a pedagogic point that whatever the cultural prescription of the object or things represented, we wish to establish their importance and particularly for the individual who took the picture. We are, to use our largest generalisation, trying to *make the lived present*, which at this stage in the development of the practice will be rather like providing a detailed map, different for each individual, yet drawing on the same signs and symbols. The more finely textured and considered this pictorial map is, the closer it will correspond to the identity of the student producing it. It will be a map which contains real, mythic and ideological understandings, insights and meanings. The point is, that it will have a significance for its producer.

(Above and pp. 62–3) Photo-story. Cockpit Department of Cultural Studies. One of our attempts to use a popular form to reflect upon practice. Original photography by Dave Hampshire

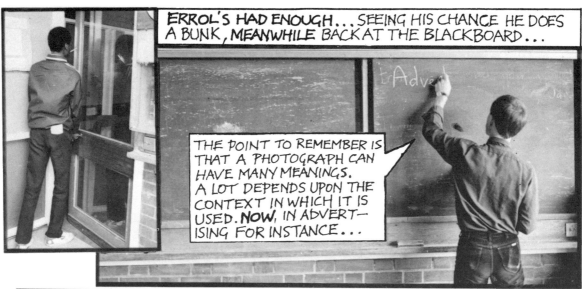

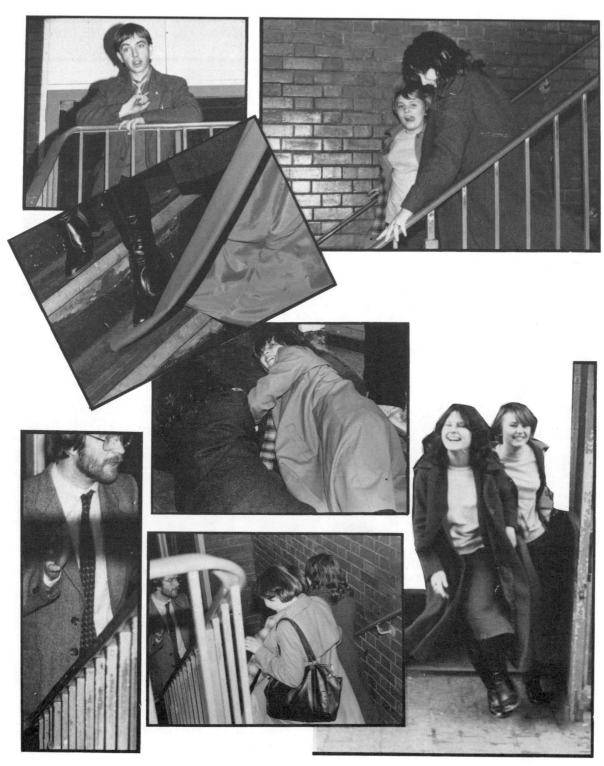

Pupils' rough layout for a photo-story about 'bunking-off' in which, by chance, the apprehension by a teacher was real and not acted

Contact sheet and one selected print from a 'weekend assignment'

Popular form and uses

We have shown that young people have no difficulty in taking up practical photography. We have suggested that popular and dominant ideas about photography and the organisation of photographic markets make it easy and self-evident for young people to start using a camera. They do this in an unproblematic way by taking snapshot photographs which is the common and popular mode of photography. But in which ways do young people understand and value the results of their snapshooting? How do young people use their own photographs? If the practice of taking photos has a common-sense basis in the popular form of family snaps, then we should expect the forms of their use to be similarly located. Prints are avidly consumed by the young people we work with. There is a constant demand for photos to take home to give to friends or family. Whatever form the particular assignment in hand takes there is this additional demand for specific pictures, which are valued in a context initially beyond the reach of ourselves and the project. It would seem then that an answer to how young people use their photographs requires us to speculate about this context. To say something of how photographs are valued in the domestic worlds of young people.

Popular photography is part of everyday life. It is located in the domestic contexts of people's lives and the photographic results are related back and refer to the valuing of relationships within the domestic world. Photographs are collected and displayed in the privileged and private space of the home. The family album, the drawer full of stored prints, framed portraits and snaps pinned upon on the privileged and private space of the home. The family album, the drawer full of stored prints, framed portraits and snaps pinned on kitchen and bedroom walls are the significant forms of the domestic photographs use. These forms are not isolated or static, they are related because photographs are circulated and displayed over time. A

print which is first roughly pinned on the kitchen wall may eventually go to make a page in the family album or be kept in the family photo archive. Prints are also circulated when they are sent or given to friends or relatives. The circulation of photographic prints and the forms in which they are displayed and collected constitute the social use of the snapshot. The overall character of these uses is their connectedness within the flow of everyday life. The making of images about selected and valued relationships that people have to each other and the world is naturalised in snapshot photography. It is part of the continuum, unseparated out as a means of representing and communicating value. Snapshot photos are built into the process of social exchange. A closer look at the social relations of the use of prints shows us how.

Looking at photos

When a set of pictures is first back from processing there is a flurry of excitement, a keen, sharp interest in looking at the results. The prints are avidly devoured, hurriedly scanned. This is a moment when the photo can be experienced as something unusual and special. It is a similar moment to that of watching the image appear in the developing tray. This first response, this first gaze holds a great deal for those who took the photos and appear in them. For this combined group there will be the interest in what the photographs represent and how this relates to the occasions out of which they were made. There will be the recalling of details of the people, places time and events, the reliving of the occasion. The prints will trigger the wider and fuller memory of what is depicted. There will also be some interest in how events, people and places have been represented. Judgements will be made about the likenesses of the print to the people present and whether the image is fair or flattering, crude or misleading. There will be the more technical consideration of whether or not the prints will come out all right.

Judgements will be made about the exposure, and colour of the print and the framing of the subject. The discussion between those present when the photographs were taken will also, in all likelihood, make passing reference to what was not photographed. The absence of certain people present on the occasion of the taking of the photographs will be noted. All these points, remarks and comments will be made as the prints are handed around and viewed for a first and perhaps second time.

The chain of circulation extends when a member of the group depicted in the prints, or, the person who took the photograph, shows them to other friends or relatives who were not present when they were taken. The photographs now take on additional dimensions as they are used to communicate to others. They will provide information about the appearance of people and places. They are used to give an impression of what has not been seen or that which has changed. In the process of the circulation of photographic prints they will be 'captioned' by accompanying speech and conversation. Points arise out of, and are returned to, what has been represented. Questions are begged and answered in looking at prints.

After the initial circulation of prints the pattern of use changes. In all probability they will be shown less frequently. The collection or set of prints from the same film may stay together simply as the bundle in the processors envelope, put away in a draw, eventually to be selectively used in an album. Alternatively, the set of pictures will be broken up and used in different ways. Favourite portraits may be put in frames and displayed as part of the ornamentation of the home, or they may be sent to distant friends or relatives. These same photos may not be looked at again for a considerable length of time.

With the passage of time the meaning and use of the photograph changes. They become historical documents which help mark the passing of time. Interest and excitement is renewed in photographs with their ageing. The viewer becomes the detective in identifying unknown or distant ancestors and locating the original context in which they were photographed. The snapshot photograph is the historical document of everyday life. Photographs gain significance as part of a related collection. They become order within an historical document. The status of such archives has great variability across users. Photographic records of families both lapse and are rehabilitated. They follow the fortunes of families and currently can span an historical period of up to a hundred years.

Popular histories

Snapshot photography has little of the conscious construction we associate with documentary, news and photo-journalist photographs. As such and in contrast they appear naive and innocent. They appear to have no detachment from their subject and context. Snapshot seem inevitably part of what they represent. This has always been a point of relegation, even dismissal of the snapshot within some professional photographic orthodoxies. There are visible and current limits on the ability of popular photography to construct critical perspectives and histories. But this is as much to do with the social relations, conditions and context of use than it is to do with any absolute convention of representation. Snapshot photography also has real strengths as the basis for the construction of popular histories. The making of persistent photographic records by working people over the last hundred years provides a relatively independent means by which individuals and groups can assess their own historical progress. The family archive has the limit of being privatised, but it also has the strength of remaining so far separate from dominant and official representation. Historical change is given specific inflection and significance by the photographic record of families and friends.

An image from a pupil's 'weekend assignment' representing a family representation!

The status of family photos

The social context of the snapshot is very stable. Collected snapshots in albums, boxes or whatever are continuously possessed within families and handed down through generations. They are rarely reproduced in any other form. Thus the snapshot acquires over time the quality of a precious object, even though it is endlessly reproduceable. The older the photographic print becomes the more it takes on the quality and presence of a relic. Like many other privately owned and treasured objects, photographs deteriorate. The fixed image degrades, the colour fades, tones are bleached and the paper dries out. Negatives are often lost or never acquired, making the print a unique object. The ageing of the print corresponds to the distancing in time between what is represented and the contemporary viewer. Memories fade with photographic prints. The physical changes in the condition of the print over time and the handing on of family albums to another generation are shifts in context which alter the meaning of the photograph. What the photograph represents becomes synonymous with the social location in which it is used. As social attitudes change, distinctions are made and noted about what is represented in older prints. In this way, the snapshot comes to be used to describe the social habits of historical subjects. Styles of dress, hairstyles, facial expressions, body postures and gestures become so many clues to be deciphered.

Young people's relation to popular use

When young people take up photography with us they are often initially disappointed that they can only use black and white. They see it as a second best to colour and lower in status. This response doesn't last beyond the time taken to make a print and take it home and the issue is rarely subsequently referred to. We've not substantially worked out why this is so, since it has not presented us with a problem. Instead we have been able to work on the assumption that the standard postcard size black and white prints which they make have currency. Such an assumption is borne out by their subsequent use and by the more general recognition that what is photographed is initially more important than how it is photographed. Young people clearly use their own photographs in a similar way to that which we have described about the family snapshot. The main feature, and for us significant difference between adults and young people's snapshots, is in what they show. Nevertheless, the currency for black and white prints is important. Without it projects such as ours couldn't develop since the cost of colour printing is prohibitive. The currency and use of black and white prints by young people has a substantial overlap with that of the parentally centred family snapshot. The difference comes in the pacing and definition of what it is important to photograph. In the family album young people are more often than not the passive subjects. Whilst young people are quite happy to stay with the form of the family album they do have a different agenda of what to include. In our experience their own albums are much wider in scope. For instance, whilst head and shoulder snaps of family members are important to include in an album, they go

Image for a 'youth album'. Young people photograph what is important to them and map out a relationship to the parent culture

alongside an extended catalogue of friends and photos of themselves. In general, the family album doesn't give much status to photographing objects in any detail. Holiday snaps, of course, contain views and amusements and diversions, but little of what is domestic and familiar gets represented.

Young people, however find no difficulty and actively set out to represent a whole range of details within their everyday environment (see pp. 72 and 73). Prints made from pictures taken in school, after school, at home, over a weekend, and in the studio, jostle together in young people's own collections. Whether they institute their own album at home or keep one with the project, the album has a character similar to that of a diary. It is a personal document, a document about what is important to them at a particular time or over a particular period. Prints take on a different use and status when an increase in size is suggested – 10 x 8 inch black and white prints are regarded as good enough to frame and display. They are often produced as gifts to parents or relatives. Above 10 x 8 inch and on those rare occasions when a 16 x 12 inch can be made the subject is nearly always themselves. These photos may also be framed but it is more likely that they are used as posters on bedroom walls. At the other end of the size scale young people will often want to make miniatures for lockets and key rings, or more conventionally for bus passes, passports and wallets. Occasionally a photograph which has common reference to a group will be produced in greater numbers to be distributed amongst friends. We have discovered boys illicitly selling photographs of girls and girls wanting photographs of boys. In general, all these individual uses of prints are highly conventional and prevalent in the culture and young people try them out. They don't last long and soon give up their interest. The one popular form that does sustain them is the relating and ordering of collections of their photos either in albums or when working on exhibition panels (see pp. 67, 115, 121, 126, 127, 129, 130). The reason for this is that edited and selected collections of photographs is the most available way of

controlling and manipulating the meanings held in relationship to what the photos represent. It is the active work on meaning that holds young people to the photo-practice.

Youth albums

Young people use photos to 'map out' a relationship to the parent culture and the culture of their peers. They photograph what is important to them and this guides their subsequent selection and use of photographs. They do require help in being shown ways in which they can order their 'map' or translate it into an available account. This is an area of complex teaching engagement with what they find important to represent. It is also a point at which the question of the present and future use of the photographic work is raised, which in turn raises the question of what form the work should take. The limits of existing popular forms and uses are reached at a point when young people want to make clearer the meanings contained in the collections of snapshots they have made. In effect, a point at which they choose to order the experiences to which the photos refer. The question of the form and use such work might have is a hard one for young people to answer. At this point in a practice they know little of the extended forms of image/text work they might use, what purposes such work may have and who, other than themselves, may be interested in it. Under such circumstances it is right that we should expect young people to be cautious of what they don't know and wary of purposes and interests outside their everyday world. It is right that we offer them a protected space in which to continue work in which the main centre of representation is themselves. The family album is something they know and can work within, it can continue to provide a

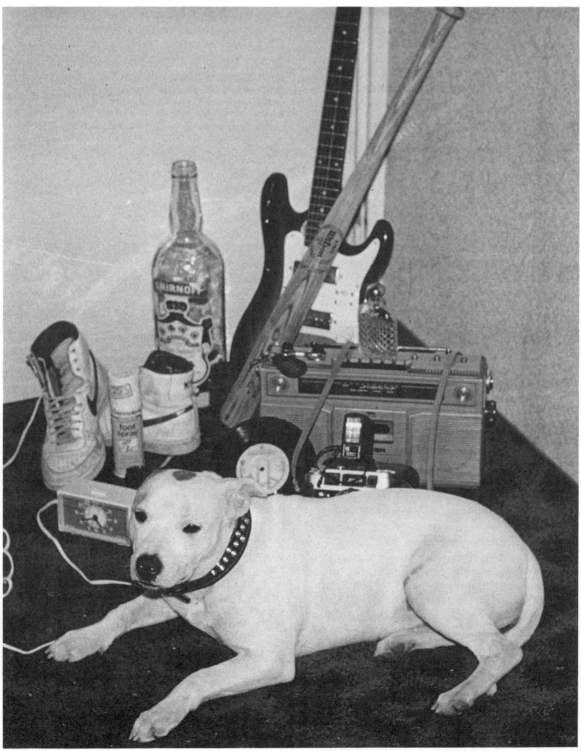

(Above and p. 73) Young people actively set out to represent a whole range of details within their own particular everyday environment

framework for exploration where the commitment is primarily to themselves and to a lesser extent their tutors. This form may not in fact actually lead young people to order prints in a photo album. It is enough that the designs and layouts of their pictures are temporarily held within a known purpose and interest.

Young people's photography and popular histories

If the family album can be regarded as the basis for potential work on popular histories, then young people's own work comes into a relationship with this same possibility at a number of points. One of the most straight-

forward ways in which this can happen is where young people make the connection between representing themselves and representing their family history (we discuss this more fully in Chapter 4 (pp. 118–21).[7] A less obvious but equally interesting connection with popular histories can be seen in the photographs young people take of the styles within youth cultures. An explicit interest in the history of a particular style is always a possible area of development, as it was in the work undertaken by a group of Rockabillies.[8] When the Rockabillies traced the sources of influences of the music they listened to, their style of dress and associated interests in cars, cruising and hair cuts, they were actively shaping a popular history. A history which importantly included themselves as a contemporary point of reference. Youth cultures contain countless submerged histories in the persistence of some styles and tastes and the transience of others. The popularity and following of particular bands is a case in point as our illustrations here show. The group Madness has been around for some time and the frequency with which some reference to Madness appears in young people's photos is quite surprising. They appeared in Mark Duke's photograph which he took in 1979, they appeared in a young woman's photograph taken at home in 1984 and at regular intervals between. It is through our somewhat privileged access to the project's contact sheets that such things can be traced. The project negatives themselves now amount to a limited archive of South London Youth Culture in the early 1980s. Many other themes can be cross-

referenced within the collection. As yet this is not something young people have access to and the possibility of a popular photograph archive remains a remote idea. Yet young people's own collection of photographs, taken over the relatively short period of a year, will contain many references to changing styles. The surface of youth culture is continually shifting and so if a practice of taking pictures is established, some of the surface inescapably becomes documented. It is often hard for young people to make these changes the subject of their photographs. Since they are within these changes at any given time it is usually in retrospect that they can spot what's happened. Sadly this is often at the end of a project. But style is a continual source and subject for young people's representation and so whether consciously worked upon or not they become historical

(Above and p. 75) References to the band 'Madness' in various young people's photographs in the early 1980s

people – or 'loners' as they are sometimes called – whose relationship to school and their peers is characterised by a high degree of separation and independence, young people organised by the friendship group have no difficulty in giving immediate shape and direction to their photography. For such young people there is a rapport between the activities and values of the group and the popular practice of photography.

What we mean by the friendship group is where a small number of young people within the larger school groupings seek out and enjoy each other's company as a way of being at school. In particular, we are describing such groups where affinity operates in relation to an activity offered to them as

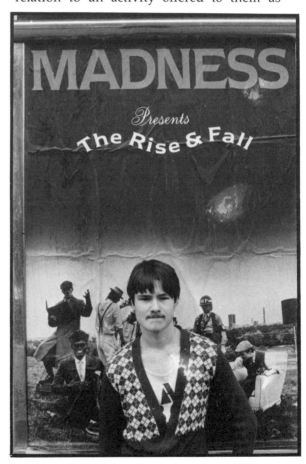

references. The history of styles and their meanings can become a focus for young people's work on representation within work on the family. A young woman, currently interested in putting together a family history, came along with a faded Boots chemist processing envelope with a few underexposed black and white pictures of two rockers in a back garden. It was her Mum and Dad when they first got married.

The different ways young people take up and use photography

Collective and social use

A recurring and always very positive initial response to the offer of doing photography comes from young people loosely associated in friendship groups. Unlike those young school work. There are clearly many forms of friendship groups within schools based upon differing affinities. As we have met such groups through photography, race and territory have been organising factors. Certainly the election of friends seems to relate strongly to the social and cultural worlds of young people outside school. This could be as straightforward as the coincidence of a group of young people living in the same street or block of flats. Yet not all young people living in geographical proximity to one another will strongly indentify with each other. Something more active and selective is at work in the formation of friendship groups which move between school and home. Territorial identification is the more cultural process which takes in a number of selective factors such as sexuality or race within a social geography. Territory denotes the process of the active creation in practical, material and symbolic ways of distinct cultural groups. In the areas of South London in which we've worked, young people actively shape territories and territories provide a location and shape for their cultural identities. Within the overlap of neighbourhood and territory young people create loose networks of friendships. It is the emphasis on the exploration of identities through friendship which gives the friendship group allied to photography a dynamic character. Equally it is the location of friendship within cultural territories which allows the group to see photography as having a collective purpose.

The character of group practice

The group practice of photography is initially successful because of the rapport between young people who create spaces within schooling to enjoy each others company and the space constructed by us in which they can elect to do photography. This means that unlike many other forms of school work which require them to attend and work as individuals, photography can be established on a group basis. In a loose and informal way tasks are shared and co-operation is encouraged by the group. Selective interest and attention within the overall activity takes place so that, for instance, one person may take more pictures and hence handle the camera more than another, who may in turn prefer to appear in more of the pictures. A similar approach is adopted by the group when working in the darkroom. One person may prefer printing, or more likely another may find it difficult at first so that pictures are printed for each other. Often two people will work together on the same prints, dividing their labour or swopping jobs. In effect, each member of the group initally finds that point of the activity in which they feel most comfortable. In watching this social process in a number of different contexts it is clear that the group is capable of being, and often is, self-regulating. An example of this is where a person who persistently avoids boring tasks will be cajoled by the rest of the group into doing something, or generally encouraged to stay with the interest in a particular piece of work. This regulation extends to the equity over who appears in pictures and later in the distribution of prints for private use. The division of labour within the group is always loose and interchangeable, although over a longer time real differences occur in skill and attention. In this as at many other points we would be involved in trying to maintain a balance and encouraging an equal sharing of skills.

The group project

The group also regulates the overall pace and flow of the photography; the attention to which moves in and out of focus, is urgent one week and low key the next. The main project of the group is social, but the social interests of the group and doing practical photography are not mutually exclusive. In fact there is an important connection at the level of popular practice. Snapshot photography takes place in leisure time and is often occasioned by the gathering of friends. One of the significant purposes of the snapshot is

Groups of friends can extend a school-based project into an evening 'club'

to validate the relationship people have, usually those within the family. The presence of a camera in a family or friendship group calls forth the animation of such relationships. Taking pictures within friendship groups is a way of expressing and recording affinities. This socially available and popular convention of photography is used by the group to demonstrate and celebrate membership of the group. The given and sustained subject for the photography is themselves. No group that we have worked with has ever found it difficult to know what to do, indeed as we describe in Chapter 3 (pp. 107–110) it has been hard to persuade a group to move on from studio photographs of themselves. The connection between the cultural interest

group and the group practice of photography is very strong.

Style as the interest for a group project

In South London during the summer of 1984, the previously low-profile style of dress of the soul-smoothy was worked up into a more spectacular style. Expensive boutiques started to appear in Walworth and Bermondsey and the local youth paraded Italian and French labels up and down the Walworth and Old Kent Roads. The style was opulent and leisured, borrowed from Cannes and, film, TV and music celebrities. In South London that summer anyone who could afford the clothes could be famous.

At this time, there were two groups in the photography project operating loosely along friendship lines. By the summer of 1984 they had spent half a day per week with us for two terms. The groups were from different schools, had different tutors, were in different years (fourth and fifth) and had carried out different pieces of work. In common they were both from the same area – a traditional white working-class community. All the young people were white and there were young women and men in both groups. In the third term style became a common and predominent interest in the photographic work. Studio sessions were regularly asked for and set up. They photographed each other and got tutors to photograph them as a group. The studio sessions easily became casual and relaxed and were amusing and productive. From the studio sessions related interests were followed up in further shooting over weekends and evenings. With the exceptions of one young man who was a skinhead, the rest had adopted lesser or stronger versions of the soul-smoothy style. While the skinhead went off to photograph his mates, the rest pursued either the related interest in body popping or in the local area and fashion boutiques where the style had been put together and paraded.

Within this close range of interest in photographing 'style' it was possible to de-

tect the related but submerged interest in sexuality. The closeness and intimacy of the group created the conditions for the representation of sexuality to surface in a non-threatening way. For the majority of the time this remained as an interest in representing conventional differences or in stereotyped gender representations, although on some occasions we did engage directly in suggesting reversals of gendered postures.

(Above and p. 79) Friendship groups and pictures of 'Madness' publicity again

Some different ways in which three young people took up photography

In this section, and a later one, we try to introduce some of the uneven and unlooked for outcomes of our approach, which for the sake of manageability cannot be fully handled in describing the approach itself. So here, be referring to the often copious notes which we always wrote up after each working session, we try to define and understand the difficulties we met. We also hope that these sections might safeguard against the impression we might give, by the very fact of presenting our work as 'method and approach', that we possess some kind of foolproof pedagogy of resistance.

Issues raised

In looking closely at how three youngsters, one girl and two boys, took up photography with us, two issues are raised here. The first, which is a broadly education issue, remains implicit in what we describe and needs spelling out beforehand. Young people in general, and perhaps young working-class people especially, are very often the victims of stereotyping. Teachers, under the stress and pressure of their daily working conditions, and educationalists who cannot usually claim such mitigating circumstances, tend to characterise and relate to young people on the basis of unexamined and stereotyped assumptions regarding their irresponsibility, vulnerability, innocence, or ignorance, for example. Clearly, these can be qualities of any individual, but we are pointing to the way they can easily become the premises upon which young people as a whole, or in defined groupings, are understood.

During the seventies some important studies of working-class schooling sought to replace psychologistic and 'cultural deprivation' theories with a new and more positive stress on the part played by class, cultural and generational experience in shaping young people's responses to school. The insights contained in this work, usefully raised to the level of paradigms in one very important contribution, (Paul Willis's *Learning to Labour*)[9] have subsequently led to a new, we could say 'radical', kind of stereotyping. Basically this takes the form of perceiving young working-class people as belonging to two types. First, there are the hostile and indifferent, the heavies. Secondly, there are those who are prepared to respect the realities of the school and the work it offers them. Respectively, these characterisations are based on the poles of resistance and conformism, the paradigms of the 'lads' and the 'earoles'. This particular kind of stereotyping inverts the common-sense, and dominant, evaluation of young working-class people's responses to schooling. This happens by stressing the informal political content and creativity of the resistant youth, who are seen as being in touch with their class roots and traditions of subversion, and by inferring a 'cop out' or accommodation to ruling-class myths on the part of the conformists.

Whilst it is clear that this was not simple intention, or the full sense, of the studies which have supported, even generated, such stereotypes, there is a related outcome which we have learnt to contest. We have often noted that these materialist analyses of contemporary schooling, and related attempts to investigate its history, can finally offer the teacher little more (apart from knowledge of course) than the most general principles for guiding pedagogy. This has something to do with the author's respect for the variability and contingency of concrete educational contexts. But it is also rooted in the terms of the analysis which can provide complex and powerful models of the social dynamics of resistance, and more by implication of conformism, but fails to take into central acount the reality of the substantial majority who occupy a mediated and negotiated position between the poles. It is the interests of these youngsters, as much as those of the virtuosi of resistance and the 'achievers' that we should respond to.

A related point is the way that resistance is seen as the province of male youth, and male

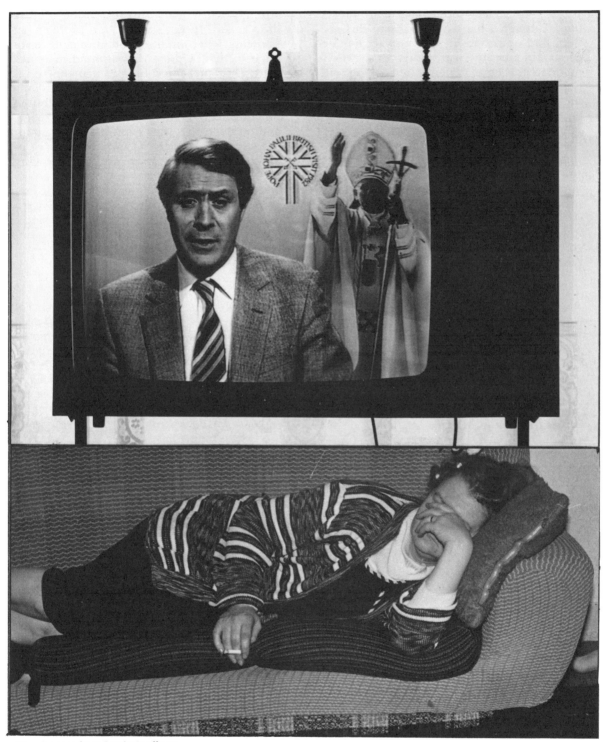

Two images from Louise's album

youth are seen as typically and overtly resistant. Through what we describe in this section, and elsewhere in the book, it has become abundantly clear to us that this is inadequate. Our experience in working with popular forms of expression and in respecting the wider, lived experience of young people, indicates that many young men are oppressed between the poles of their peers spectacular resistance and aspiration. Also, some young women are much less 'invisible' and more active in relation to both of them than the current terms of the analysis often seem to admit.

The second point which arises here strictly concerns our arguments about what is involved in a cultural practice of photography. We meet questions about how young people can use and value their photographs when institutional definitions of their value as art, as proof of technical competence, as schoolwork, or as a hobby are not imposed. This is a discussion which we will return to later when considering what is involved in developing more extended and independent photo projects.

Louise, Tony and Marco

The three young people who figure in this part of our account all belonged to a larger group of ten. They worked with us for one year within school, for a second off-site. They each had difficulty in taking up the opportunities which we believe, and many young people confirm in practice, our projects put before them. In a way this seemed to be of a piece with their lack of confidence, even in resistance, which characterised their position in school in general. But there is an important difference to take into account. Work with us is optional and self-elected. And whatever difficulty they found in the work they returned time and again to find some more to do. The two boys related

strongly to cameras and technique. Louise didn't. All three shared the problem of knowing what to take photographs of; or of what in their worlds they wanted to represent. They presented big problems for us as teachers. On the one hand, they continually fell short of fulfilling the tasks they set out·to do, however modest and carefully chosen, and on the other, they expressed a liking for the work even in the face of an absence of anything to build upon. In the following extracts from our notes we see this problem and our responses. It is important to remember as you read them that Tony, Marco and Louise keep turning up for sessions, enthusiastic, expectant, wanting to 'do photography'.

Tony

Tony's film shows that he has only taken a further six shots since last week. He didn't even load up the fresh roll of film that I gave him to take home last week. 'I'm no good at thinking of photos to take,' he said. Marco had shot two films, he ruined one by trying to unload it without pressing the release button on the camera. The other has been used up on shots of the interior of a supermarket.

Tony

To avoid the impasse which Tony faced (no negatives to work on) we gave him a camera and sent him off with Colin to take some photographs. There were plaintive cries of resistance from Tony. A refusal to go to the West End with a reel of twenty exposures to do a kind of 'image and context' exercise. Refusal to take up the simple alternative of taking pictures according to their own choice, (. . . rushed and getting desperate) Colin complained that Tony wouldn't co-operate.

Tony and Marco

(A session in which the tutor started working in the studio with these students; an exercise in photographing objects, trying to work with their interest in technique and 'effects'.)

We want you the choose any object you like in this building and photograph it so that its purpose is less and less clear . . . I demonstrated by using an ashtray, showing how by lighting and angle I could make it look like a flying saucer. When it came to their choice Tony said he would use the ashtray! I ruled this out, saying they had to choose, Tony said it was silly . . . Marco was not particularly enthusiastic . . . he maintained a dead-pan expression. His main interest was in the actual close-up lens and the teleconverter which he spent a long time inspecting. Tony said that his Dad had bought him a camera. He too was interested in the technical side of the exercise.

Tony

Tony brought his new camera to show us – Minolta 35mm SLR. He had used it to take pictures in his own home, an exercise we had set him the previous week. As usual he had taken very few pictures, and those were shot at the wrong film speed. Marco was slightly peaked about Tony's new camera and spoke (for about the hundredth time) about the new Practika on the market and did I think it a good camera. Neither of them had brought in any objects to photograph as I had asked them to.

Louise

She did not show this strong interest in the technology and neither did she have such a pervasive difficulty in taking photographs. Her difficulties arose more in the area of valuing and using her photographs which were predominantly taken inside her family's flat, mainly in the living room, of a dog and her young nephew.

Tony

The difficulty which these three had in getting their work off the ground is not, in our view, a problem which strictly concerns photography itself. Their difficulty is the more

general one of finding a practice of self-representation and expression. Lying behind this, it seemed, were difficulties which they shared in marking out generational identities for themselves and in sharing the collective symbolic practices of other youth.

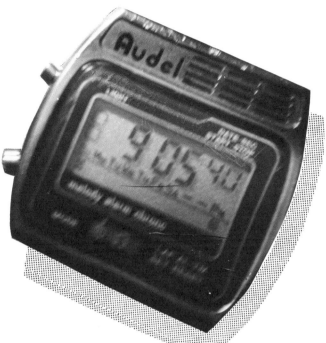

'A digital watch watch . . . which plays a tune'

In a way, Tony's photographs are eloquent about this. Three of his recent photographs indicate the limits of his material culture. A close-up of his digital watch, the kind which plays a tune. Then, the photo of one of his parent's ornaments: a tiny replica of a radio-gram. In response to a number of 'assignments' where he had been asked to take photos of his and other people's lifestyles, or of objects and activities which were important to him or others close to him, his snaps were limited first to his model cars, a train set and a video game, and secondly to nearly everyone of his parent's ornaments, holiday souvenirs, and the framed pictures of their living room. It was at times difficult to remember that he was the classmate of young people who took pictures of themselves playing pool, smoking 'spliffs' or in exclusive peer group contexts. Tony's third picture is perhaps the most eloquent of them all. It is the picture taken from the high rise flats. Having exhausted all he can perceive as possible subject matter within the interior,

'A tiny replica of a radiogram'

and in the absence of the cultural practices and sites which many working-class youth typically make so much of, Tony shoots a picture of the distant world seen through his window: a bird's eye' view and a snowscene in one.

At school, Tony's responses to lessons moved between a desultory tolerance and a passive resistance. He was often frustrated with his own efforts to carry out work. The world he represented beyond school appeared to centre upon private community based amusement or in sharing his parent's culture, watching TV or playing video games. In itself this is by no means unusual or remarkable, but most of his peers would place these activities in a context of other images which referred to all those ways through style, humour, and use of free time, by which they marked out a critical, even

oppositional, relationship to popular and parental cultures. It was hard to see how Tony was selective about the way he inhabited and consumed these cultures. There seemed to be a difficulty in separating out a partisan image of himself as a young, white, working-class male which led to a problem of privileging everyday things to photograph.

If Tony wasn't one of the 'the lads', neither was he a conforming, ambitious school pupil, out to do well in the system, or working the system. So neither was he able to represent the way he imagined or aspired to a future identity by taking pictures of things which he already possessed or which pres-

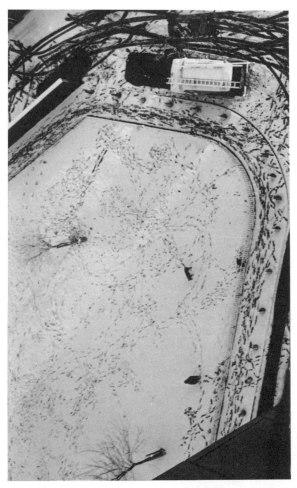

'A bird's-eye view and a snowscene in one'

aged future goals: textbooks, posters of heroes, smart clothes on their hangers, record sleeves, a piece of furniture or whatever. Yet the material symbols of a popular, parental culture, and the youth market commodities which he pointed to in his photos were soon exhausted and, anyway, hardly set him alight. Yet in the absence of anything else, say the less domestic, more arcane aspects of working-class culture – fishing or collecting, for instance, or the more specific and collective cultures of youth – Tony has, perhaps, little to choose from. We have seen that Tony's point of connection with photography is the technology. This is what sees him through and keeps him interested. He talks about his camera rather than what he uses it for, he buys gadgets and attachments for it regardless of definite needs for them. It would be difficult for him to value the possession of a camera on the simple basis of the rate at which he takes pictures. When the camera is available he is quite ready to lend it to other students in the group, he lends it proudly. His possession of it is perceived quite accurately by other students as the possession of a piece of prized technology in itself, rather than as a practical resource. 'Who bought that for you, your dad?' 'Yeah.' 'Man if I could only get something like that at Christmas' (this was mid spring). 'Have you got a colour tele?' 'Yeah.' 'A video?' 'Yeah.' 'A tele in your bedroom?' 'Yeah.' In this way the camera was added to a list of leisure commodities. This is surely where photography meets Tony's interests, at the intersection of technology and leisure.

Marco

Despite similarities between Marco and Tony's positions, Marco has, however, found two subjects for his recent photos which temporarily lead him out of the impasse of what to shoot. Both involve an adult neighbour. He first took a number of shots of the man next door with a model sailing ship which he is building, plus some of the workroom and the plans for the boat. More rec-

ently, he has taken shots of the man and a friend exercising with heavy weights. This fitted in with an earlier preoccupation of Marco's in taking pictures of martial arts' exponents. He had problems in seeing this through as it transpired that he did not practice any martial art himself and found little mileage in continually photographing the school judo club. He was eventually reduced to copying photographs which he found in martial arts' magazines. This interest was short-lived under such conditions. It reappeared, as it were, in the form of the man next door. Prior to this, Marco had suffered much the same difficulty as Tony. It is Marco who we meet in our notes quoted above as having spent one out-of-school assignment (ostensibly directed towards representing the signs of lifestyle), taking pictures of a friend filling supermarket shelves. This in itself was the single departure he made from taking pictures of his mother, father, sister and the family living room.

It is a fact that when we equip students to take photographs of their everyday lives, what we do is cause them to consider the meanings that they find there. As we stated at the outset, we ask them to take seriously and actively any value that is normally suppressed, left 'out of court', or taken for granted. For Tony, this has brought him 'lens to face', as it were, with the degree to which he is contained by the practices of a parental culture. Marco, while having like Tony a very remote and diffuse relationship to anything like a specific youth cultural practice, finds something of significance in the leisure activities of adults. Two adult males with decidedly masculine hobbies.

This brings us to a further point which has made the development of a cultural practice of photography difficult for Marco and Tony. It is the question of the use to which they can put their photographs. Neither of them has been able to use their photos to communicate to others – no matter how familiar the 'message' might be or how local and small the audience. They have not been able to give their photographs a place and work to do within their social relations with others. It

From Marco's album

would be true, no doubt, to say that their photographs do have a small and immediate audience, and are accorded value within their families. But further and more extended circulation amongst members of their own generation has not been possible. This again has a lot to do with the absence of extended friendship and peer groups within their social worlds. It also sheds some light upon their relating to photography primarily through the technology. We have seen how they both met a problem in knowing what to take pictures of. They fell, in the process, into taking pictures of a narrow range of culturally prescribed objects in which they found some significance and another set to which they were indifferent. Boredom and frustration soon set in here. Their second problem was to find a form and use for their work. Two related issues. They have both worked on compiling their own albums with as much enthusiasm as they ever show for a practice which involves engaging with social meanings, and all the signs are that these are viewed by them as forms of 'school-work';

something akin to the 'project folders' with which they have become so familiar there. The 'project folder' is itself an aspect of a once 'progressive' pedagogy which, due to lack of connection with real uses in the pupils' social relations beyond the school, has been more or less incorporated into the range of alienated school-work. It becomes increasingly easy to see, then, that for Marco and Tony the point of producing images, the very manipulation of the technology and handling of the physical process, becomes the centre of their attention. It is as if they would prefer to be technicians without the responsibility for initiating work and without concern for its eventual use. This, of course, is a bizarre inversion of the educational project which we are trying to generate. We are having played back to us an acceptance of, even a preference for, the kind of hierarchised division of labour which we, and many young people, seek to avoid.

It was due to a recognition of this at some level that we set Marco and Tony to take photographs of simple objects at odd angles – an arid and orthodox practice for many young people, as it is limited to technical manipulation with little or no connection with the students' more compelling interests. It was in fact the kind of exercise which deadens. the response of many students when they are introduced to the practice of an expressive medium. It may have given Tony and Marco the kind of security within a limited task which they welcome. Further, it allowed them to operate the technology without needing to consider anything beyond the veracity of the image in the viewfinder to that yielded by the unaided eye. Pedagogically, it was hoped that they would simply be able to take some photographs; to have at a basic level a practical involvement with photography. It was an attempt to meet a *sine qua non* of our approach.

Forms

This strategy is remedial. We are pulling back to find a way into working with these two students. We are seeking for an approach to the practice which they are in a position to take up. In a way, this makes our work with them commensurate with what has happened in their general schooling. We originally met them in a remedial English class and they are both rapidly dropping out of the schooling system to be caught in the net of YOPs and 'life skills' courses. Yet we can understand the problem differently. What is understood in schooling as a problem of intelligence quotas, motivation or deprivation is given to us as a problem concerning their place in the dominant culture. This is a culture in which the identities of working-class children and youth are prey to a range of ideologies. Ideologies which, through the institutions of family, school and the media, have permeated everyday consciousness. Given a particular conjuncture of ideologies and institutional vehicles to carry them, the possibility of a collective and resistant, or at least 'distancing', stance within dominant cultures be-

comes untenable. In such cases, the values of that culture are imperfectly, but adequately enough, reproduced as they are carried in a bemused and passive way by young people like Tony and Marco. They exist in a grey area between definite options; between building oppositional and critical myths on the one hand and aspiration on the other – however contradictory with knowledge born of experience – to secure a future on the terms offered.

Photograph by Louise

Louise

In recent weeks, Louise, working off site at our centre, has taken more photographs, more readily, than either Tony or Marco. What we have learnt of their way of relating to photography through its technology and commodity form does not hold true for Louise. The points we make about their position within class and culture do. Yet both sets of issues have to be looked at from the point of view of Louise as a young woman, if we are to get some understanding of the forces working against us in developing a photo practice with her.

Photograph by Louise

A familiar sight on a Wednesday afternoon would be Louise sitting alone in a room adjacent to the darkroom leafing through her photo album. She would stop at a page every so often to dwell on a particular picture much like someone scanning a newspaper, looking for items that interested them. Without sustained pushing from a tutor towards the darkroom, developing room or studio, this is how Louise would spend her time. The same would hold true for her use of a camera. She would seldom ask for one. But with some cajoling and insistence on our part she would usually take one, bringing it back a week later than asked with photographs taken. She would never press to develop the films or get on with printing it up. She seldom expressed a strong interest in seeing what she had done. Typically, she would hand over her camera on arrival, not a word spoken, and move to take up her place with her album or perhaps a magazine found lying around. In turn, we would suggest, probably several times, that she got on with developing her film 'Yeah, Yeah, 'orl right,' would be her sharp response as she moped off to do it. You could literally count on one hand the number of times Louise has smiled during a year of Wednesday afternoons.

Apart from five or six frames taken on a recent CND march which she went on with her brother, all Louise's photos are taken within her parent's council flat or on the landing and stairs outside it. Most are taken in the main family living room. The pictures are very loosely framed figures often situated at the edges of the frame, sometimes half in and half out. It is often difficult to decide who or what the central subject is meant to be. The backgrounds are arbitrary, one or another slice of the domestic clutter of the room. Occasionally, as with the shot reproduced on page 56, her photos can be printed up without any further cropping to resemble the studied informality and flat patterning of 'arty' exhibition prints. Not that Louise would be interested in this if we pointed it out to her.

The pictures nearly always show other women, sisters, aunts, Mum, women neighbours. They sit around, watching the tele, reading the paper, putting their feet up, or are seen through a doorway tidying, cook-

Photograph by Louise

ing, washing. Children are nearly always around. There are a fair number of shots of Louise herself, probably taken by her brother or a friend. She usually 'loons' about in these shots, debunking the fact of having her photo taken. Louise has changed considerably over the period we have known her, from a scruffy, raucous girl always shouting at others, calling them slags and wankers, into a much quieter and contained person. She dresses much more carefully, often wearing a tailored tweed jacket, pencil-line skirts with side vent, stockings instead of knee length socks. Her hair is often freshly washed. Yet in her recent photographs of herself, she still presents herself as a clown or as subordinate to a child, or the figure trying to hold the dog still for the camera. Never has she done what is so usual for many other girls; make images of herself as a glamorous female.

Commentary

Louise, like Tony and Marco, is something of a loner. At school, in the classroom, she was not part of an active friendship group. She did not appear to 'go around' with a distinctive group. When the basis of the group changed from timetabled English in school to an option off site, Louise was the only girl to follow through. Continuing with photography on this basis was not a straightforward 'easy option' for any of the class. The other, as it were competing, options were school based and non-examinable, ranging from Health Education to Metalwork. Continuing with photography also meant a disruption of daily routines, travelling over lunch and getting home later than usual. In our experience the novelty of the journey 'up West' would soon wear thin with most pupils. For many it would never have seemed preferable to the secure patterns of the school day and the won spaces for having a laugh. A number of students who opted for photography initially foundered on this basis. They found excuses to stay in school when it came to it. Further, most of them had learnt by now that whilst we admitted contents into lessons which were usually ruled out, we also made them

work. We stayed close to them, we were usually just around the corner whatever 'diversion' they tried to take. The lack of other girls in the group did not seem to worry Louise. It certainly did not stop her coming. She hardly spoke to the others in the group, neither the black group nor the two white boys. She never made a fuss or problem about the technical or practical nature of the work that she was expected to do.

A major similarity between Louise and the other girls we have worked with is found in the centrality of the home, the duties of childcare and a share in the continuous round of domestic work which occupies them daily. These factors – both social and physical – make up the site for most girls photo practice. Louise may not celebrate a dominant image of femininity but she does represent the female gender role in the home and the visible lack of a symbolic practice outside it. Louise, then, shares with Tony and Marco an everyday reality contained predominantly within the home and cultural practice centred on the working-class family.

Photograph by Louise

The massive difference which gender brings is that for Louise some relation to domestic work and childcare is always present. For Tony and Marco there is a kind of cultural vacuum partially filled with popular, commodity-based, leisure practices. Louise's world, as shown in her photographs, is a world of activities and one containing social relationships in which she has a real part as a woman amongst women. It escapes, at least as something to represent, the symbolic poverty of Tony and Marco's world. This has to be why Louise took more photos, more readily, and had a strong interest in them – even if of a very private kind – when they became prints in her album. On the other hand, it is her gender which protects her from Tony's and Marco's almost obsessive concern with the technology. She saw the technology as a means to an end and would probably have liked to have had it made simpler, if it were within her power. As she said, she liked taking photographs, quite liked having photographs, she wasn't 'mad' about any of it, she just 'quite enjoyed all of it'. She certainly couldn't see any mileage in boosting her self-image or forging an identity through being seen to possess and use a sophisticated photographic technology. This is a male preserve; part of a more general ideology which associates masculinity with the possession and control of the means of production. Yet this very ideology, working its way through the boys' consciousness, is the basis on which they sustained their attempts to take photographs. This wasn't open to Louise and not available to us as a way of relating to her.

Commentary: Tony, Marco and Louise

Unlike the black group, which we discuss later and which came to resist us in order to protect a way of working that was developed to the stage which most immediately satisfied them, Marco, Tony and Louise present us with a more complex situation. Nevertheless, it is one likely to be met often. They are embarked on a project, structured by us to be based in the representation of their worlds. But there is little in their worlds in terms of objects, artefacts and practices to which they attach strong personal, symbolic meaning, through which they project aspects of an identity or to which they have a charged response. Instead, they chart the features of a sparse landscape. To celebrate the life they lead there is not easy. Neither do they have a place within cohesive groups of young people outside the family. They do not participate in sites of symbolic practice beyond the family and private leisure consumption within individuated friendships. This means that there is no available social basis for the use of photographs, no circuits of communication, no collective identities to reinforce and contribute to. This latter point also contributes to the difficulties they find in being able to envisage the possibility of themselves making representations for a wider audience. They have no partisan message; feel no comparability with the collective cultural formations of youth which exist around them.

In order understand the position of Tony, Marco and Louise as much as possible we only need to remember this, that for the hundred odd students who have participated in our projects since we began to monitor them, the photos they take always contain a range of very definite signifiers. In any list there will be Hi-fi, homemade sound system, a range of posters, adverts for bands, concerts, discos, photos of recording artists, film stars, erotica, the tokens of football fan, sports equipment, pictures torn from magazines, of customised cars and motor bikes, fashion plates, book jackets, comics, musical instruments, etc. In terms of activities and practices there would be dancing, hanging around a cafe, amusement arcades, being with a group – a gang or 'the lads' (usually shot in surroundings consciously or accidentally connotive of the 'urban ghetto'), combing a prized hairstyle, smoking a fag, a tatoo, a pierced ear, kissing someone of the opposite sex, making defiant or obscene gestures, posing next to admired objects – a bass speaker or holding a pool cue, being suggestive of sexuality in some way, and so on.

It is clear that many of these signifiers speak only of male identities and practices. The more limited range open to working-class girls is found by them amongst the ubiquitous shots of domestic life which dominate their films, as in the case of Louise. While the majority of students work from this base to become more and more selective and controlled in the meanings which their photographs carry, Tony, Marco and to some extent Louise hover at the base line. These markers of a position within a culture, the visible signs of selective consumption, hardly figure in their photos. Tony shows us a few leisure commodities with a popular youth orientation, sitting amongst his parent ornaments and decorations, the TV and the video. Apart from the passive practice of consuming a dominant culture, no activity is ever represented by him. In fact people hardly figure in his pictures at all. The same holds true for Marco with the addition of his recent interest in his neighbours' hobbies.

In terms of our own education project to develop a means of cultural expression with young people, we have here something like our own remedial situation: young people whose sense of generation and self is under-developed and submerged in the commodity based and parentally centred forms of a popular culture.

It is, however, our overall project which has led us to see this problem and begin to understand it. It is certainly a recognition which challenges, through complicating, any polarised ideas about working-class youth and their culture being based on the simple axis of conformist–resistant and even absolute distinctions around gender and race. A pedagogy with which to respond will be a new and extending task.

Images of a 'parental' culture

3

Cultural Resistance and Cultural Expression

Evidence for generalising about young people

Our position in organising photography projects for young people affords us a privileged insight into their worlds. This comes to us through having access to the photographs they take. Looking at their photographs and talking about them with young people has always been one of the most extraordinary aspects of the experience of running the projects. Over the last five or six years, on a weekly basis, we have looked over the regular production of contact sheets made from films taken at a weekend or after school. These contact sheets are stored in files with the negatives. They are filed by school or group in chronological order and referenced by date, photographer(s) and subject. On average, each file representing one group's work for a year, will contain between fifty or sixty sheets of negatives. Each sheet of negatives will comprise thirty-six frames. So a completed negative file will store somewhere in the region of 2000 individual 35mm frames. Currently we have in our archive twenty-five such files. This amounts to somewhere in the region of 50,000 photographs taken by young people in South London between 1978 and 1984. The entire collection of photographs reproduced in this book represents a tiny proportion of the total we had to draw upon and it is difficult to give the sense of the enormous number of images we have become familiar with. What makes our relationship to the archive special

is not only that we can range over a large number of photographs, but that we are able to recall a lot about them as well. A contact sheet taken from any file in the collection will trigger memories of the people depicted, who took the photograph and many of the details surrounding the circumstances in which the photographs were taken. It is as if each of the 50,000 frames is an index to a larger account. Fifty thousand or so recorded events containing details of the lives of young people we have known.

It is on the basis of what the photographic archive shows and the larger experiences to which the photographs refer, that we can claim to know something of young people's worlds beyond our first-hand knowledge of working with them. The intimacy of the snapshot has given us 'secret' glimpses into privileged aspects of their private lives. Without any disclosure or betrayal of trust it is possible to 'read' the archive, to generalise from the 'evidence'. It is possible to say something about both differences between and a common way of life amongst young people.

Growing up working class – the terms of reference

For both good and bad reasons there is currently a very keen and sharp critical response to social classification. It is our experience, especially professionally, that it has become very hard and at times impossible. to achieve any kind of consensus in generalising about groups in society. It has become clear to us that within educational and political discussions a whole set of received definitions are being challenged and reworked in an exceptionally complex way. The primary challenge, in our view, is centred on the received body of thinking about social class. There is at present a special crisis and confusion in the ways of thinking about the nature, composition and status of the contemporary British working class.[1]

We have an overriding reluctance to move into the arena of theoretical and political debate in this account. In fact we're not going to. But we do, unavoidably have to skirt around the edges of the discussion in order to make sense of the context of our work and its wider aims. Indeed we also need to generalise about the young people we've worked with in order to make sense of their varying responses to photography – in particular the phenomenon of resistance.

Growing up working class – the evidence and the issues

1. Common conditions

If, as we have done on many occasions, you were to spend half a day or more looking through files of contact sheets, you would form some very definite impressions about the material environment and culture of the people who took the photographs and the people who are depicted in them. What the photographic record shows is continuous with our experience of living and working in the South London districts of Peckham, Walworth and Bermondsey. We know that the majority of young people we have worked with will live with one or possibly two parents in council accommodation built anywhere between the 1890s and 1970s. In the London Borough of Southwark, which includes the three districts mentioned, 80 per cent of people live in council property, the majority of it being flats. There is a very high population density. Much of the accommo-

dation, including that most recently built, is inadequate or in need of repair and improvement. Some of the most gross examples of the deck access barracks are just south of the Elephant and Castle (see page 127). Apart from the flats, the environment is filled with industrial buildings spanning the same period from the Victoria wharfs on the Bermondsey river front, now being converted into guarded luxury apartments, to the corrugated windowless warehouses of the new and empty industrial units. With the exception of a few surviving manufacturers, Sarsons Vinegar and Peak Freans to name a couple, there is little in the way of industry. Like other inner city districts the council has become the largest single employer. The majority of the employed travel out of the borough to work in the service industries of Central London. By all traditional accounts these three districts are solidly working class. The public environment is, as it has always been, poor and uncared for. It is the shabby continuation of a Victorian industrial area.

This material environment is the ever present backdrop to the photographs young people take when out and about in the area. All the young people we work with have to make their own lives against this common environment of walkways, car parks, stairwells, derelict building plots and littered, dog soiled open spaces. This environment is still sensibly understood as a working-class district. The majority of those in work are in either manual, service or low-grade positions of wage labour with no property other than those of personal possessions. This is the common economic condition where the sharpest boundary lies between those who have employment and the unemployed. For most families there is little to fall back on if the wage stops or fails to keep pace with rising prices. Under such conditions the shift into poverty or criminality are real possibilities. Economic insecurity is not new in these areas, it is a feature in their creation and has given rise to criminal subcultures with a very long history.[2] We have often come into brief contact with the outer surfaces of criminality as young people describe the experiences around their photographs.

Within the range of labour – casual, criminal, securely waged and unemployed – there is a common pivot around the immediate presence or lack of money. For the securely wages there is perhaps a possibility of extended monthly credit, more associated with the middle classes. But for the majority the pattern of spending power still hinges on whether the weekly wage will last until the next one.

This common economic position in relation to purchasing power is present in the photo archive in as material a way as the built environment. In the photographs young people take in their homes, family possessions are the given background to a further set of photographs and are as often the subject of them.

The importance attached to certain orders of possessions is very strong with young people. It is possible to rank these according to both market pressures and persuasive interests. Hi-tech audio-visual equipment is virtually a universal interest with a continual ranking and checking out of quality against manufacturer and cost. In most cases, the installed equipment belongs to an older brother or sister or parents. Apart from these obvious aspects of youths' interests in the machinery of popular culture there is strong interest in the overall quality of the interior environment. Most young people who are prepared to photograph their homes are intensely proud of the decor and possessions of their parents. This valuing of the home as the primary social site and repository of value and possession is still part of a common condition and culture. The family is still the dominant form of social life. It is, however, its privatised and privatising form which, linked to wage labour, leads to and maintains the social experience of division, exclusion and subordination.

2. Social and cultural differences

Within the general economic and cultural context which we've outlined as working class, there are a further set of determining conditions affecting young people. The groups of young people we work with come from an extraordinary diversity of races. Both the old and new imperial and colonial routes have and continue to lead people of the world to London, to find work, make homes and settle. This process of movement of people has a historical dynamic and is continually in change. At present, in our area of South London people of Afro–Caribbean descent make up the largest group of the age range in schools where we work. It is, as we stress, continually changing and hence generational. But our point is that race is both a positive condition of cultural difference and a negative condition of social division. The black community is an especial target for overt forms of racist abuse and attack and the dominant institutions carry and reproduce racist ideologies and practices. Under such conditions, young black people especially experience a sense of enforced negative (i.e. subordinate) difference from their white peers and combat it by a positive insistence on their own sense of cultural difference. The structure of the family has decisive effects on the way social divisions and differences as well as social cohesion and affinity are reproduced. The extended family still provides a structure of social support and cultural affinity. At the same time it maintains separations between different races living in the same areas. Extended family relations provide a social structure for most young people in the area where we work.

The family is also an important context for the third equally determining condition affecting the position and outlook of a young person – their sex. Less than a quarter of the young people we've worked with during the project were young women. This is in part initiated by an early history of working in single sex boys' schools; that we are men, and that within mixed schools girls often perceive photography (not surprisingly) as male gendered. Nevertheless, it was clear to us that these young women experienced exclusion and subordination on the basis of their sex. The photo archive shows how their social movement was more restricted to the home. The home, and in particular house-work and childcare are present in their photos and largely absent from those of young men. Young women experience sexual harassment and the pervasive threat of male violence. They are, generally, socialised into accepting male authority, prerogative and power. This has all the recognised outcomes of maintained social passivity, isolation, limiting aspirations and restrictive practices. It is also combated through social solidarity and positive assertion of female difference leading to separate association from men.

Class, race and sex

We know that there remains a great deal to be understood, as well as an enormous amount to be changed in the existing relationships between and within class, race and sex. We cannot be clearer than we have been and accept that we don't have political answers or complete theories. What we have outlined is our understood position in which a social system driven by economic exploitation creates subordinate classes and multiple oppressions. We understand that patriarchy and imperialism are built into the system in ways which are complex and historical.

These very general parameters of social and political theory have been important in our practice because they have helped us understand the specific subordinations of the young working-class people we've worked with. They also point towards an understanding of the resistance many of them have to schooling and society and hence in our work with them.

Making the transition from school to work

Young working-class people experience society's contradictions in a very acute way. They experience a society in which most things are apparently and potentially avail-

able to them. They are encouraged to want the best there is of a material culture. They are constantly presented with the idea that almost anything can be satisfied by material consumption. They know that power comes with property and possession. It is reasonable for them to expect that they will participate in this society of consumption. At the same time they experience a continual lack of money. In relation to consumption, they are themselves economically powerless and experience the lack of money in relation to the family's or parent's limited purchasing power. They hear and see the rhetoric of plenty for all but experience the reverse. They are encouraged to admire the powerful but are themselves powerless. They experience the competitive nature of success and realise that not everyone can be a winner, yet are then expected to accept various kinds of institutionalised and social failure. They are expected to have lower expectations, to accept a lower status, to work for less reward and to be deferential to various forms of authority. In particular, working-class young people are sensitive to the process whereby their aspirations and hopes are closed off or regulated by the discipline of compulsory schooling. In the face of the multiple contradictions of society and a system of power weighed against them, they resist. They resist not as a conscious protest and not on the basis of an organised politics. They resist instead as themselves, as a part of everyday life, as part of their social practice.

The ways in which young people resist is open to great variation in form, subtlety and power. But resistance is a mode of cultural self-empowerment in a context of structural powerlessness made by being compulsorily schooled and economically dependent. Resistance is a way of dealing with negative authority and limiting conditions. It is a way of temporarily reversing situations, of making something out of nothing. Resistant social actions create self-esteem and group solidarity. Resistance is, however, only resistance, it doesn't substantially transform the conditions which give rise to it in the first place. So resistance is also a limit. It represents something like a stalemate in a continual war. This is very visible and reaches acute proportions in working-class schools. It presents very particular problems for teachers who wish to get close to what working-class students experience.

Resistance in schools

In schools teachers have to struggle daily against the competing interests and scepticism of their students. Working-class students bring their experience of a wider reality to school, where it provides a basis for collective strategies for resisting the demands and overtures of schooling. They resist the organisation of their time and attention in ways which are at odds with the impelling present and the concrete logic of being young and working class. They are met with the soft policing, social engineering, and efforts toward moral compensation which make up much of a teacher's work. The negotiated ground between resistance and containment is the site of a very refracted struggle between class values and cultures. In this struggle the teacher's position is largely maintained by their being identified with the school as a whole and its connections with other state institutions which serve the working class. The striving for the student's acquiescence to authority depends as much upon the material and symbolically loaded organisation of the school timetables, bells, and tannoys, physical divisions, rules, codes and sanctions, and the value-laden role play of the institutional heirarchy as much as upon the skills of any one teacher. It has often been the case that, in an effort to move closer to the students' expressed interests, the teacher proclaims some degree of open solidarity with the students' resistance and by implication a remoteness from the core values of state schooling. This can rapidly involve a teacher in an attempt to deny their objective role as an accountable and validated representative of the dominant culture.

Regardless of how principled such a willed separation of the teachers and the institutions values may be, it will almost certainly be rejected by working-class young people as a basis for co-operation. Such a stance loses the teacher credibility in their eyes and further diminishes their precarious claim to a reasonable authority. The students can be relied upon to assess realistically the teacher's position along the lines that the teacher has been given a job to do, a responsible middle-class job, and that job cannot be to bite the hand that feeds them. If the teacher thinks and acts as if this is really on the cards then they must be soft, a mug, or worse, some kind of rootless subversive. This view is given to the students by much more powerful agencies than the individual teacher's assertions or actions. It comes as part of a popular conception of 'education', it overlaps with common sense, and most immediately it is carried by a thousand popular images of the 'idea' of the teacher. At the same time, the teacher who relinquishes any relationship with the dominant 'idea' of teacher and turns his or her back on a socially constructed reality will suffer, in the eyes of their colleagues and managers, a deprofessionalisation. They will become marginalised, unsupported and unresourced in their work by the school hierarchy. This will be a proof of the students' assessment of the situation; one which, from their side of the desks, they will help to bring about.

Our relationship to institutional resistance

The answer to the problem of being seen by both students and other teachers as abdicating an institutional role is provided in our approach in two main ways. First, we always engage with the students lived experience through a concrete and disciplined practice: photography. We claim our authority here, as teachers who possess practical skills and who, given the students' respect for the necessary conditions of practice, are more than ready to impart those skills. This position has all the advantages of the practical discipline over the academic in stressing concrete and useful outcomes over deferred goals and abstract, class-based qualifications. It also involved, as we have said repeatedly, a body of skills which have popular currency and are by no means necessarily tied to the narrow definitions of what is valuable as school-work. Secondly, whilst we put ourselves in the position of having subordinate knowledge to the students in respect of the objects of study which they nominate, we do not naively place ourselves, even were it possible, into their class cultural frame of reference. We maintain, and often elaborate on, a distinct presence as members of a different class cultural fraction. So, having ruled out a magisterial role in relation to the students (represented) lives, and needing to avoid being passive spectators or what is made present or celebrated, we have to see the perspectives and meanings of our own life as an important resource.

The larger aims of our approach

1. Overall direction

There is, of course, a link between our view of basing a representational practice on what working-class young people privilege, and our view that it then becomes necessary to open up and relate more of your own values to them. It is a very different pedagogy from that entailed in teaching for exams where the teacher has to maintain the position of speaker and arbiter of an objective realm of knowledge. It is not that we reject the pedagogic authority which has developed over the historical reproduction of academic disciplines on every occasion. Our point here is that the academic subject and its hierarchies of knowledge and teacher-based pedagogy is an inappropriate starting point in popular mass education. In our view, it is oppresive to working-class students. Whilst it may aim to increase the community who can participate in the received wisdom of historical

knowledge, it actually functions to exclude and fail the majority. In this sense we are neither 'liberal progressives' nor 'deschoolers', even though we would like to see the institutions of higher education made fundamentally democratic. In recognising the failure of the dominant pedagogy successfully to engage working-class young people on terms they value, it becomes necessary to elaborate an alternative.

We also recognise that the state schooling system acknowledges its own failure in this respect and continually accommodates the widespread non-engagement with academia. It does this on its own terms by posing either the vocational curriculum or a series of compensatory and remedial programmes. Such programmes and curricula have often been produced in the face of a 'crisis' of the relationship between schooling and employment. The current 'crisis' is precisely in these terms where a vocational curriculum is being updated and enlarged to accommodate and adjust to mass youth unemployment. The construction of state schooling into the academic and vocational affects the way any cultural practice can be taken up within it, and our practice is no exception. Photography is most often located as a practical subject in the old liberal and examinable curriculum. Our stress on the practical nature of photography projects has often been sought out by teachers responsible for running compensatory or remedial programmes. Currently there is a growing interest in photography as part of vocational training. Effectively our work has been rationalised within either set of terms. We have, however, never seen this as setting the aims for our work even though it has often set limits on immediate goals. We have tended to see our work in schools as bargaining for a space and the best conditions we can get in order to try out ideas and possibilities with young people. We should perhaps explain next our general aims in relation to such ideas and possibilities.

2. *Resistance and popular culture as a starting point*

We remarked at the outset of this account that we had 'discovered', as it were, an extraordinary powerful and dynamic relationship between working-class young people and the production of photographic images. The basis for this, we said, lay in the connection between the currency of the photograph as a powerful carrier of meaning and the process whereby young people explored possible identities in their transition from school to work. We would now like to connect this idea with the processes of resistance.

Resistance is, in our view, a mode of social action, it is a way of having a positive identity in a context which is oppressive. It is a way of 'subverting' the structural relationship of subordination within given limits. In fact as far as young people are concerned it is about testing what the limits are without finally or completely being able to break from them. As such, much that is resistant is by nature highly coded, obtuse, elliptical, elaborate and consciously deceptive. Oppressive authority maybe the motor of resistance but it is not its clear object. A great deal of resistance is aimed directly at figures of authority, for example, teachers, parents and police, but there is, we reckon, a deeper sense of oppression which resistance also expresses. This is the sense of being within a *system* of subordination which threatens continually to encompass the limits of what it is possible to be in society. This more pervasive condition of oppression means that resistance is equally a more pervasive response. It is not only activated in reply to overt conflict with authority, it becomes a way of being in society. It contributes to a sense of positive self and is therefore constitutive of cultural identity. This is, for us, the point of connection between resistance and photo practice. For if, as we've shown, photography can be the basis for an exploration of cultural identities in an educational context, then part of the exploration will be, for working-class young people, related to resistance.

The character and content of contemporary youth resistance

Part of growing up working class, or black or female, entails living under conditions of oppression. The specific forms of oppression require always that specific individuals be subordinate to a dominant system of authority. Growing up of necessity involves socialisation, which for working-class young people, black people and women is to be soicalised into subordinate roles and identities. However, growing up and being socialised also involve the recognition of contradiction and the experience of social and sexual conflict and antagonism. So resistance is also part of socialisation. Resistance is produced in the specific sites of growing up, traditionally in the working class community, in the schools, in the family and in youth subcultures. Resistant identities are not separate from dominant identities for young people. They *live* a number of possibilities, they explore unconfirmed roles. The content of resistance is related to the given form of oppression. So girls will resist through the dominant versions of what is female. They will explore the possibilities entailed in the identity offered by femininity.[3] Working-class boys, both black and white, are confirmed in their dominance over girls by the gender role of male power. They resist through the patriarchal ideology of physical superiority which leads specific individual boys to harass girls and for boys as group to dominate socially. At the same time black boys experience the oppression of racism. This sets up the possibilities for resistant identities to be explored through race and gender. One current version of this is the exploration by black boys of the male images and ideas of being beyond the law, in fact of being the 'outlaw' from a white society. White working-class boys explore the opposite male image of being at the centre of power, or more generally of social cohesion which is contained in nationalist ideology. In all three cases what young people are doing is using elements of a dominant system of oppression to resist the effects of being oppressed. Our view is that such a process is a continual part of cultural activity.

Positive centring on young people's experience

Our primary aim has always been to develop ways of centring working class, black and women's experience as the basis for educational work. As we have spoken of it so far this is not as simple as it might appear. Young people do not necessarily recognise sympathetic overtures on the part of their teachers, as we noted in our discussion of resistance in schools. It is almost certain that they would find any overt reference to oppression as either patronising or perverse. There is simply no direct way of identifying such an interest which would avoid their reasonable suspicion. There is also no institutional context in which centring on their experience avoids their resistance. They are resistant, as it were, to any attempt to make resistance the obvious subject of educational work in situations where they have no control. It is not possible for them to 'give up' resistance simply because the teacher announces that she is on their side.

Nevertheless, the aim remains a central one and it is clear that certain forms of cultural practice allow for a negotiation between cultural workers and young people to take place in relationship to what young people value as a form of resistance. Photography as cultural practice is one such example.

Engaging with resistance

In attempting to centre upon young people's experience within schooling we have been confronted with their alienation from the educational process. Our aim in centring on their experience is precisely a strategy to overcome this overriding alienation. But, we hasten to add, we don't do this in order to encourage their adjustment to the existing state of schooling, but in order to establish a basis for an educational process to take place.

We have already noted that it is perfectly possible to establish a buoyant photo practice in relation to young people's interests. We have further noted some of the characteristic ways such a practice is taken up. Our subsequent aim is to enable (to structure and lead) the practice to develop – for it to become more complex

Selecting from contact sheets within an extended self-directed project

Stages in the development of a practice

Over the last six years of working on the photography projects we have, on several occasions, attempted to formalise a method of working which relates to the interests, pace and developments within groups. Each time we have attempted this something new or unexpected would occur to contradict our conception of a sequenced and identifiable set of stages. Our current thinking is that it is

(Above and right) Weekend work and humour. Making the 'lived' present? See below

not possible to formalise a system of teaching or way of organising photography as a cultural study. At the same time we don't think all our effort was wasted in the attempt. What we have ended up with is an understanding about a characteristic set of stages that occur at various points in the practice. The nearest we have got to sequencing these stages as a method is a follows.

First   To establish a practice in relationship to the popular currency of photography. This is understood as making selections from snapshots on the basis of personal interest. At one time we called this stage 'Making the Lived Present'. What we meant was a way of raising what is normally lived and taken for granted to the level of possible subjects of attention for photographic work.

Secondly   We saw this process becoming more focused so that selection in both the

taking and printing of photographs would lead to a more deliberate process of 'Celebrating' an aspect or relationship to lifestyle, i.e. we saw a stage, often related to using the studio, of making positive representations.

Thirdly   We planned our own role in 'Engaging' with what was being celebrated. This was a specific point of pedagogic relationship where we thought it was possible to 'problematise', or make them think more about what was being celebrated. As we look at it now this was a rather arbitrary moment when we expanded the focus of the work and set them on a more complex course. What we think now is that this process is happening all the time, the attempt to formalise this as happening at a particular stage shows clearly that an exact method cannot be constructed. In the attempted method, we planned that through 'engagement' the practice would move on again to a fourth stage.

Fourthly We postulated 'Articulation' as a stage where a conscious practice of representation had been achieved. Again we think that articulation can happen at many points in a practice and is not necessarily a highly developed stage. An obvious example of 'articulation' would be documentary projects of whatever nature where there is a degree of planning and forethought in the representation of a chosen subject. We reserved a further term for what we took to be 'complex practice', which within the attempted method would allow articulation.

So, finally we proposed a *Fifth* stage which we posed as 'Reflexivity'. In our view, reflexivity as we posed it never actually occurred in any established or sustained way. Again we now think it is more a question of elements of being reflexive, or young people being reflexive about work they had done. However, reflexivity was our title for a critical and responsive practice which, at best, would be organised and sustained by young people on an independent basis. In a way we modelled the concept on what we aimed for in our own practice as cultural workers. It was the much struggled for praxis.

The reason why this scheme of stages doesn't add up to a method and why the delineation of stages doesn't match what happens in practice, is largely about why reality cannot be made to fit neat theories. It is also, in a much smaller way, due to the fact that the resistance leads above all to strategies of divergence from centralised aims and structured approaches. This is, we think, more than demonstrated in the example that follows where we discuss a style of teaching. In this example a group of young black people are finding it hard to know how to develop their practice and we are finding it harder to tell them.

What our scheme of stages should perhaps indicate is the quality and character of the cultural practice we aim to achieve with young people. The problems met in practice, centrally those of relating to specific resistances, also lead us to a further set of considerations about the cultural and institutional context of the practice. The discussion of the limits and constraints of various further locations for photographic practice forms the basis of chapter four.

Teaching style – an example of engaging with resistance

'Affirmation of identity': possible closure of project

We look here at problems we experienced in finding a framework in which a group could extend their practice beyond a very developed use of the snapshot. As in the previous, similar section, the account is based very closely on notes made at the time.

The account concerns the work and interests of a group of six, occasionally seven or eight, young people who worked with us through their last term at school and slightly beyond. Some of the group had been involved with us on continuous projects for two years, many of them classroom based and structured as part of formal lessons. Others were more recent 'students'. At least one of the group has maintained a social and occasional working relationship with us ever since and is now working as a colour printer in a commercial processors.

We met the core of this group when we introduced practical photography into their 'extra' English lessons. (These lessons were known as Language Development and provided for low achievers.) We contributed to four out of their ten weekly sessions for a whole academic year. During this time we worked in their classroom at the school. For a second year, their fifth year at school, the group travelled 'off site' to work at our centre

(Above and p. 103) Two of a friendship group's studio portraits discussed on page 104

some three miles from the school. They did this for half a day per week as a 'Social Education' option. At the time of the session described below, the majority of the group have just left school. They are in limbo between school and possible futures of unemployment, youth training schemes or further education courses.

In preparation for the afternoon session with this group their tutor prints up three negatives on a large format. They are to be shown to the group as soon as it arrives and were taken during recent 'studio' sessions. The studio is a large classroom which has been transformed with the aid of a large plain backdrop and flood lights. The tutor chose these shots to print with the aim of stimulating the students' interest in the results of those sessions. He chose a more or less 'classic' group portrait, a picture of two girls in the group embracing, and a third of two boys presenting themselves as fashion models.

The large scale of the prints was intentional. We wanted to give the images all the status and connotations of the exhibition or publicity print, or perhaps the 'double page spread'. We also wanted to give the students some idea of the kind of photograph they could make in a studio situation; to give them a real idea of the range and degree of detailed information which could be achieved and the kind of mediation through use of lighting and arrangement of elements which was possible. Basically, we hoped to give them the idea that they could move beyond a snapshot practice while dealing with the same subjects or contents – their own and their friends images. If this could be done we could then look towards evolving new forms of production with them which went beyond their personal albums. The simplest of such outcomes would be a sequence of connected and constructed photographs which could be exhibited, or perhaps a pamphlet or poster. At the most formal we would envisage them making a contribution to an exhibition on youth style.[4]

Responses

Five students turned up that afternoon. Three of them appeared in the photographs which had been pinned up. Their initial responses ran very much on the lines of gender; on how well the images served to represent them in terms of dominant stereotypes. One of the girls screamed with embarrassment. She didn't like the dour expression she had in both the photographs. She was embarrassed by the implied relationship between herself and the boy on whose lap she had sat when the photo was taken. He, on the other hand, was pleased by the image. Danny, the young man who stands at the back of the group was stunned and open mouthed when he saw it. He said nothing for a minute or two – just drunk in the image. All of them laughed and took the mickey out of the two lads in the fashion shot. They asked if they could have the pictures. We explained – as we frequently have to – that we had to keep them as part of the project work but they could make more prints for themselves. Our main point was to ask them to take take some more shots in the studio. They should now try to go beyond the ones in front of them. They should try to take pictures that avoided the meanings they dislike in the present ones and develop those they could already see and did like. We added that they could certainly have copies if they paid for the paper at cost price – say £1 a sheet. Interest evaporated . . . they pushed to get out their negative files and to print up some 5 × 7's. This is where the currency continued to lie for them. They wanted numbers of pictures to take away and show to others at home. Danny, in fact, printed up one of the negatives which we had used for the large prints on a minute scale in order to fit it into the plastic window in his wallet.

Directly, then, the strategy appeared to have failed. The mediative qualities of the large prints were by no means lost on the group, but they did not lead them to want to break with the snapshot and the album. To expect an immediate response and take up of newly posed possibilities would be to ignore the social relations of the group, which were now fully part of the organisation of the work. For instance, the two young men seen in the group shots were newcomers. They had not been regular members of the group over the years but had frequently figured in their photographs. They had recently been brought along to the 'studio' sessions and were now working themselves into a position to take up a practice along the lines of the regular group. Despite having seen these constructed studio shots of themselves, their main interest at this point was to borrow cameras to take pictures across the week in their own time. The others in the group were keen to encourage them in this and enthuse about the possibilities as 'old hands'. The way the group sustain interest in this way and actively work to extend the practice across their social group is, we would claim, a real achievement. As long as the practice is sustained and our working relationship with them continues, the opportunities for taking up and articulating the very responses to the images will recur. It is very much a matter of waiting for the right conjuncture of factors. Many of these are beyond our control as they depend upon the patterns and rhythms of the students lived experience in relation to the ongoing practice of photography. The point is to keep creating the opportunities and providing the conditions which are in our control.

In the darkroom: a pattern of work established

The studio sessions where the shots were taken and the act of printing them up for the group were part of their tutors' efforts to develop new kinds of work with the group. They had worked consistently and with enthusiasm for over a year at this point, but the way they had worked was beginning to show its limits. During this period each member of the group had shot anywhere between five and fifteen rolls of film in their own time. They had turned up regularly one afternoon a week to develop and print their

films. Almost without exception they now take their pictures in a number of distinct sites: the school grounds, after school, a youth centre during the later evening, a few at home, and some on the walkways and balconies of the estates where they live. The pictures show friends (certain ones recurringly), boyfriends, girlfriends, older (and very occasionally younger) brothers and sisters, cousins, uncles, and a few family groups. The subjects either pose in highly conventional ways – basket ball stars come pin-ups, 'hard men' on the street corner, blowing smoke rings, a lone male figure walking in the street, collar turned up, coat flowing, or are 'snapped' having a laugh, mock fighting, smoking in the toilets. Mum, Dad, elder sisters are seen in the living room posing around the sofa.

Over the period most of the group have learnt how to print well enough – when they wish. At the beginning of a darkroom session they move rapidly to select negatives for printing up. They resist and avoid much discussion about these selections. They see the criteria as uncomplicated and obvious. They have two basic criteria; first, who is in the picture, a certain friend or fancied person make more impressive photos than others. This involves an element of how they are shown, their stance or expression. Secondly, if there is a choice to be made between a number of shots of the same person, it is usually made on whether they look 'hard' or 'sweet'. Technical factors are still subordinated to this kind of intimate cultural valuing of the images for most of the group. There are, however, increasing signs that, as they become more familiar with the quality of images which it is possible to produce, they are becoming reluctant to print bad negatives.

The group's drive to produce prints on the basis of these values is well illustrated by notes made may a tutor after a darkroom session.

They were all pushing to get to the darkroom having got some new negatives. The lads moved straight to work, sharing enlargers or on their own. In some cases they had an audience of 'visitors'. (As often happened pupils extra to the group turned up with them.) One of the 'visiting' boys and later two girls did some printing themselves under a regular students supervision. The atmosphere became one of intense production. They worked efficiently and at speed, co-operating over the use of the trays and the wash, speeding around to exchange enlarger filters, focus finders, cut paper, etc. The atmosphere was relaxed, with occasional outbursts of humming or singing, as people tend to when 'off guard' and absorbed in some activity. There was the usual bantering and repartee. The girls were gently chiding the lads, especially Chris, for their mistakes and failures. In return they boasted even more about their abilities. As we neared the end of the session – which lasted for three hours – the whole group somehow organised itself into a team for final washing, drying, and even trimming of prints. The 'visitors' got fully involved in this, taking their lead from the regulars. I found myself by the sink, squeezing prints and handing them to Chris . . . to Danny . . . into the dryer. (I literally found myself locked into this role in what seemed like an inexorable process.) Something of the order of fifty prints of generally good quality were produced. In the room next door they were trimmed by Trevor and handed out for their owners to put in their albums. Trevor and Tony (both visitors) demanded albums of their own . . . assuming a place in the group. There was a clamour to borrow cameras. This arranged they bounced out taking their albums with them.

These notes give us something of the flavour of a good session with the group. We can also see the limits. The darkroom is the place where negs are turned into prints to be returned, as soon as possible, to the friends and relations who appear in them. We have already noted how the photographs are taken in the everyday sites of home, club, after school and housing estates. Now, via the darkroom, they will be returned as prints to be consumed, talked and laughed about, perhaps admired and pinned on a wall or just stuffed in a pocket soon to disintegrate.

Darkroom work is seen above to take its place within the circuit of representing meaning, producing and using. Photographs are made, very selectively, of particular individuals and groups, their 'image', stances and activities. A further selection is made as they are printed. The prints find their way into the students' albums while other copies are circulated amongst the peer groups and communities which the students belong to. In terms of the understandings we speak of in this account this is a very real and valuable process. The students photo practice is based upon popular forms, it is firmly based in friendships which exist beyond the school where the practice originates. The work they do has concrete social outcomes and it is tied to known and definite uses. The compiling of the photo album is the most formal aspect of the practice. It is the form which we have offered the students for giving some initial shape to their continuous recording and celebrating of identity. Yet, over a lengthy period of time, the 'circuit' has become so well established that it is now tending to close off the possibilities for development. It is becoming hard to suggest other ways of working, to see new uses, to propose conventions other than those of the simple realism of the snapshot, to speak to audiences other than the most local and immediate to the students.

In a way, the very success of establishing a photo practice which is based in the students' everyday experience and uses popular photographic currency with a group of students who have a well-defined cultural identity has created its own problem. The group has come to protect the value it has found in the practice as it stands. It has (almost literally) come to *possess* a practice. The students came to resist any initiative, avoided any possibility, which could have led to breaking the circuit of use and value which they had established.

An attempt to move the work on: setting up the 'studio' sessions

Our first concerted attempt to break the circuit had been to ask the group to contribute to an exhibition on youth style. We had pointed out to the group that their photographs nearly always moved in the area of representing peoples 'style' and lifestyle. We told them that our exhibition was relatively weak and unspecific in the area of black people's style, yet we could sense that amongst young black people there was a whole spectrum of identities and attitudes being expressed through style; that it was a complicated scene. The group could easily build upon what they were already doing to produce some worked up exhibition panels. From our point of view this would also be the point when we could collaborate with the students to provide forms and conventions with which they could begin to articulate the meaning of the symbols and celebratory motifs which were already established in their work. They voted with their feet. No one turned up at the session immediately following this discussion. When they did return the week after, it was to push the terms of the work back to immediate practical tasks. The tutor noted:

> In this session I wanted the group to think about my suggestions for a more structured piece of work again. I'm going to suggest that they take their interest in photographing friends further by setting up some 'studio' sessions where they can get friends along and take pictures of them under more controlled conditions. I will replace the 'Style' exhibition proposal with this. It will simply be a way of moving to the same end but in a way that builds upon established patterns of work and interest. They have rejected the idea of exhibition form and public representation; yet they may be keen to increase the power of their representation of their peer group. This can be done by going beyond the snapshot into constructing shots in the studio. Perhaps this process, the demand

for greater control over the expressive techniques which will be put at their disposal, will lead to them seeing more outgoing uses for their photographs. Ahh, but the best laid plans . . . :

When the group arrived there was great pressure to print and process everything which had been building up over the last few weeks – a set of negs to print and three films to process. More than this, Chris also brought with him some black and white prints of his sister in her nurse's uniform – one portrait shot of her and one group shot of her with her class at nursing school. He demanded to copy them. This was for himself, not his parents, they were important for his album. I suggested that he made time another day; that he could come in one evening to do this work. This seemed a way of reminding him that he could expand the amount of time when he used our resources and of extending our practical working relationship. He was lukewarm about this. I struck a bargain with him: I'd help him copy the prints if he'd help set up a studio session back at school.

We did the copying towards the end of the session and others in the group came to watch. They were impressed by the apparatus – copying stand, lights, the metering and concentrated care that seemed to go into the job. Keith asked if I knew where he could do photography at college instead of signing on. Could they continue to work with us after they left school – was this possible? So, in the event, we did have a discussion about future work, but it was about notional futures of studying photography vocationally and about continuing with a hobby after they had left school. It was occasioned, as so many of these conversations are, by successful collaboration around a practical task and an enjoyment in using the technology involved.

What about the studio session for friends? They had been enthusiastic about the idea when I first proposed it at the beginning of the session. But now, just before they left, it came to making some arrangements. I

Studio photograph. 'Style' and having a laugh with the group members, Burberry scarves, which were virtually badges of membership pointed out that they would need to line some people up. We couldn't deal with too many people at one session, especially to start with. They should limit the number to about ten. Also the 'models' would need to be available over lunchtime. If they saw to this I would arrange for a suitable room to be made available in the school and bring the lights and other equipment. OK?

'Its not on sir. They'll go mad . . . fighting an' all that. You'll have half the school in there . . . we won't be able to control it. (Then, tongue in cheek.) You know what black people are like . . . primitive!'

Some four weeks later, the first 'studio' session at school did take place. We held it immediately after school. This one, and a subsequent one, were not too successful. On one occasion some of the people who had been lined up had been let out of school early, leaving us with a very reduced group. Some key figures were absent. On a second occasion we were plagued with technical disasters. Finally, summer term exams over, the friends who the group had been seeking to photograph started to accompany the group to our centre. The photos we have looked at here come from one of those sessions.

We can see that even this revised idea for refining and extending what they were already doing was meeting some obstruction or, at the very least, continued to be seen as in competition with valued and established routines of work. Chris's demand to copy snaps of his sister was a particularly ironic twist. We have often spoken of the importance of family snaps and photos showing a student's and their family's history, especially if they can be brought under active consideration alongside the pictures the students are currently taking. Many times we have asked students to bring along' old family snaps as part of a piece of project work. Most often we had a poor response. Chris highlights this at the exact moment when new initiatives are being pushed through. In fact, throughout the whole period described here, when negatives were being produced both out of school and in the studio, it was still the former which the group were most interested in printing.

Some points about method

The position of this group in relation to the idea of a developing practice is instructive. Their entrenchment in a way of working, and the difficulty we as tutors had in generating developments with them, should not blind us to the achievements of these students and the potential of the pedagogy. The main lesson is not to see the developmental schema through which we have described a 'method' as determining. The concepts upon which the method is based are seen as leading to one another and overlapping. They can work out in practice this way too. More often than not, however, no such lucid and linear development is found in practice. Each project has its own conditions and, depending upon the students involved, different class cultural meanings, values, and responses are brought into play by an assignment or exercise. The sites of practice are very important here. What kind of school or other institution is involved? How do students come to the work – as school-work or under some other definition? What is the group's predominant attitude towards schooling; hostile or compliant? How is the project related to the curriculum or subject? Whatever the situation, it is unlikely that the conditions prevailing at any moment – whewhether conditions of response and understanding or material ones – fit the 'textbook' requirements of a 'method' schematically presented. It would be quite wrong to read it in this way. In the case we have just looked at, we see how radically different the pace and direction of the practice can be from the idea of a linear progression. We should also see, as of paramount importance, that some important educational processes have been initiated, even if the goal of 'articulation' has not been reached in any obvious and substantial way.

As it is described, the situation is one where eighteen months into a project with a group, tutors find themselves adopting a teaching strategy similar to one proposed in the early part of Chapter 2, 'Developing a Photo Practice'. This amounts to taking the negatives from the students last shooting session and returning them to them as finished prints. We do it to speed up the turn around of images and to generate their interest in the meanings of the image as a priority. The difference in the latter case is that we selected no more than three from a possible hundred or so and printed them very large. But the strategy remains basically similar to the introductory one and the motive is too. The really positive point to grasp here is that we were trying to move the group on from a point in their practice where it has been well worked into their social relations. Their introduction to photography was, as it is with all our groups, based upon a valuing of the popular currency of the photographic image; we admitted the private and domestic use of the snap into educational work. We also recognise and see the limits of its use; its confinement to and recording of a narrow range of adult centred events – the holiday, wedding, party, etc. The students in this group have reworked their use of the photographs – and the attendant form of the 'album' – around their specific generational interests. For a small group of young black students in South London a little of the democratic potential of photography has been realised. It is only its tiny scale and the fragility of the conditions which support it that make it a modest and invisible event rather than the beginnings of a challenge to dominant representations.

The group have arrived at their practice by a tortuous route. We started to work with them in their English lessons. An introduction to practical photography within the context of school brings a range of constraints on what can be practically managed and on what photographs can be taken. At points we had to stop taking photographs altogether and moved very close to a kind of 'media studies' work where we analysed images.

The students, working through carefully prepared workcards, wrote and discussed about photographs. Later, the work had to be moved on the timetable and taken off site, yet the majority of the group stayed with it. At the present time, full-time general education has ceased for the group and it has changed in composition. A core of long-standing members attend more or less regularly, and a newer, more peripheral group is forming around them as friends who come along, borrow a camera and learn to print. A group which started out as school based, set up as a remedial class, then a timetabled option, is now, as they move into unemployment or training, a friendship group attached to a photo practice. The practice is partly locked into the less formal, cultural practices of the group and their peers which takes place on territory to which we have little or no access.

They are by and large a group whom schooling has failed. They have left unqualified and disaffected. Yet during their last two years of schooling they took up a practical form of expression and communication in close connection with their particular experience of the world. They did not break with this practice on leaving school – they wanted to see it continue. The next task for us and them would be to find the conditions for maintaining the practice as pressures from the outside world build. Access, resources and forms of association beyond established institutions are begged. But the implications of what has happened here are important. On a fragile basis and within a context of disadvantage and resistance to structured educational provision, something like a model for a continuing educational process can be seen here. We have to stress the possibility of developing a cultural practice with young people with whom we have a pedagogic relation, which connects structured work to everyday experiences, and cuts through institutional divisions between school, work and unemployment. This is an educational potential glimpsed.

4

Developing Photo Practice: Social Action and Institutions

We've seen how important it is for young people to hold on to the images they make and how difficult it is to insist that they are, first and foremost, materials which belong in school. It seems that the very motivation and interest that led to their production in the first place also demands that they are returned to the informal social context in which they were made. This is something we can understand from our own experience. But it also means that, as teachers, we have to come to terms with the fact that photographs of friends, relatives, objects and activities, can never be simply formalised as school-work without denying much of their active social character. It's not on to claim the records of someone's immediate social reality as an educational resource, to sit between the exercise books and the work-sheets. However much we have wanted at times to 'move work on', to get a mountain of snaps ordered and arranged to prove to the students, the school, or maybe our frustrated selves, that a record is being made or a text constructed, we've had to remind ourselves of this or ignore it at our peril. For most young people, consigning photos to folders, to be used later, or displaying them in corridors and classrooms is no substitute for taking them home and circulating them among people the group of whom they choose. In the past we've found strategies for resolving the tension between these competing uses, such as always making two copies

of a print – one for school and one for 'personal' use – or dividing up a session in the darkroom between project work and 'own time'. But we've also thought that these strategies probably only serve to avoid a real issue in the long term. In the end, we had to see that it is only a minority of kids who are prepared or able to see school as a very meaningful place where their work can be formally presented, evaluated or appreciated. To circulate and have a laugh with their photos is something else and an irrepressible informal process within the culture of the school. Neither could we deny that for the majority of the kids a much stronger interest was in taking their photographs home. They could see a project situated within school as a useful and supportive place to make images but they saw the destination of their photos as elsewhere; home, peer group, club, and local territory. As an example of how school can have a real and practical relationship to young people's worlds, this can't be bad. We could assert that this aspect of our work is the practical achievement of an educational principle, and there must be something in that. But more importantly, it is something that happened, that we were party to, and in observing it many times were led to new thoughts and initiatives.

So, regardless of the fact that we set up Cultural Studies projects with the aim of doing innovatory work *within schools*, the results often left us looking, with the kids, more earnestly out of the windows. We imagine that, within any one project, the intensive and absorbing photographic work with all its attendant talk and decision-making must have been some of the more engaging work which the group did at school. But at the same time it revealed the remoteness of the school as an institution from the social worlds of young people. Other young people, when defined as the 'rest of the school', did not represent an audience to address for most members of our projects, and the use of their photographs within the school, whether as study material for use in other lessons or as part of the school's organised cultural life, was never high on the agenda. These were areas that they occasionally co-operated within deference to more teacherly requests. The lesson we tried to learn from this is that our approach releases a sort of dynamic which is basically inimical to discrete curriculum reform, and suggests instead that we have to look beyond the school to other institutions in the communities in which young people live as the next stage in building cultural practices with them. At one level this dynamic is running back and forth between the school as a place of cultural production and the communities around it as the sources of meaning and experience which the kids choose to express. But here we have been trying to describe its larger movement which is like an underlying current which steadily pulls us away from school as the single adequate site for young people's photography.

We think this happens because it is not only the content of photographs which is important to young people, or for that matter anyone else. It is not only what and who they represent but where and to what effect. It is the social activity of showing, sharing and communicating with photographs which increasingly becomes important as young people's involvement within a project grows. In a way, this is the popular and everyday currency of the photograph, in which our approach is initially based, reasserting itself. It continues to be a major way in which kids value photography and they resist its closure as school-work.

Shifting levels of resistance

In the last chapter we looked in some detail at an instance of this resistance. We described how we recognised this as both away in which a friendship group took up photography as something of real value in terms of their cultural and social lives and as close to their celebration of a racial identity. We also related how we struggled with what we experienced as a closure in realising our larger educational aims. We have come to understand what happened in our work with this group, in many ways it was a paradigm experience for us, as a shifting of the ground on which they resisted the dominant forms and logics of educational work. We were called to remind ourselves that in working with lived and popular forms of young people's experience, we were working, in many cases, with themes, myths, and realities in a culture of resistance. Just because we can find ways of doing expressive work with young people who resist school and formal educational practice, it doesn't mean that they have forgotton who they are, what makes sense to them, and have thrown in their lot with every idea we may have. At each developing point in the work we do with a group or an individual we need to ask ourselves a number of questions. What purpose does this new form, technique, or assignment have? How are the kids likely to see it? What kind of cultural form is it a part of? If we don't ask such questions they will certainly ask their own. If they don't see any sense in the answers from where they stand, then they will resist the developments in question as being formal impositions on their expression.

As teachers, we have our educational aims and we look for ways to achieve them. And it's from this basis that we respond to what the young people that we work with choose or refuse to represent and speak about. But in negotiating the work with young people who have by no means conformed to the imperatives and promises of schooling, we cannot anticipate many of the outcomes. We often cannot know in advance how they will receive our suggestions about what they might take photographs of, or about how they might mediate and use the photographs they have chosen to take. The points we have been making in this chapter about the checks we suffered in trying to contain too much within the institution of school alone prepared us to meet, and take seriously, further and more broadly social levels of resistance.

So it was that in a series of meetings to review the work we had been doing, and to discuss a new year's work, that we first considered the initiatives that we will soon go on to describe. At those meetings we clarified for ourselves that if we were committed to working with young people, to gain an active voice and some power to address and constitute audiences within their communities, then we were bound to become involved in more than the alignment of the single institution of school to those communities.

We have tried here to trace our own route through to this recognition but we are aware that there is also a much broader tradition of thinking about education, which stresses a similar point in one way or another. There are many possibilities as to what might be involved in an education which was responsive to the demands and interests of working people and a need to dissolve the boundaries between school and community. In thinking about this many people have seen that this entails the notion of continuing education. It means seeing an educational process as something which extends well beyond the years of formal compulsory schooling. At its best it also suggests more than seeing the school as a fixed community resource, or the community as merely a source of educational materials. It can, and should we think, take on the possibility of a more casual, flexible and dynamic relationship between everyday life, cultures, change, even conflict, and education.

In our own work we have felt this to be important not only because of a need to have places to meet up with and work with young people outside school (although the school is operating as the main base of practice), but also in order that young people can sustain and extend their photo practice when they leave school. Facilities and support are needed as their conditions change and the central place of the school in their lives is replaced by the new realities of work, what passes for work, unemployment or training and Further Education. It is precisely at the points when young people begin to anticipate the end of full-time schooling and the questions of futures arise in a pressing form, and as the complex transitions towards adult identities overtakes them, that an initially school-based practice that is social in character should have a continuing value and purpose.

So beyond the work we have attempted in establishing an approach to photography in schools, we came to the further question: what would be involved in enabling young people to develop extended and more continuous forms of cultural practice which they can control and which are not tied to dominant purposes? In terms of photo practice this led us inevitably to consider the nature of young people's access to, and position within, cultural and educational institutions. What expressive demands will current institutions meet and what degree of self-determination will young people find within them?

We can start to look at this by seeing how some of the young people who worked with us continued an involvement with photography.

Getting a job

A few young people who have worked with us have found jobs connected with photography. They soon experience the specialist divisions of labour within the photographic industry, where the 'creative' is always someone else's province. Theirs is the hard slog from the dogs-body up, knowing that 99 per cent of the way is littered with dead ends – working as glorified messengers for studio photographers, or watching a glazing machine all day, knowing that you could be doing the same thing in three year's time. This is a hard apprenticeship to photography; if it is an apprenticeship at all. Of the young people we know pursuing these routes, it is clear that the wage labouring routine is not easily related to any notion of their own use of photography. Photography now uses them.

A hobby

But what of the group, the friends and mates, the class who followed a project through together? The obvious way a group of young people may pursue a practical interest is as a hobby. Also, many popular pursuits of working-class people in particular have over time developed into institutional organisations. National networks of institutions have developed around what are basically informal social interests. The camera club is the case in point for photography. It is an institution which gives shape to individual interest, provides scope for the acquisition of new skills and frames a community of interest. Unfortunately, this general characterisation can belie a different reality. In fact we can't imagine the young people from South London who we've worked with having much of a positive relationship with these institutions. Even the version of the camera club, where it is little more than a means by which men can indulge sexual fantasies of domination within nude modelling sessions, would cut little ice with them. Any direct expression of sexual interest would quickly be ruled out of order. Membership could only be gained by using the codes by which a pretence of artistic interest prevails over such practices. In another version, artistic interest is elevated to the ultimate goal of photography. In the camera club the genres

of great photography are marshalled for members to mimic and display. These crude reflections of dominant ideologies extend to a technical interest in photography which, in the camera club, can reach highly fetished proportions. Endless gadgetry is tried out and stockpiled in the pursuit of 'quality' and novelty. It is ultimately ironic that a community of interest which is primarily social in character should take these forms within an institution where the basis of practice becomes individual and competitive. For young people who want to maintain a social practice, the camera club is likely to present another closure.

Further education

In seeking a close relation to the popular and often resistant interests of young people, our work cannot really have a vocational basis. In some ways it relates to a kind of antivocationalism as kids express it through a concern with the here and now and resist the logic of working for deferred futures. But in a general way we support and encourage entry into Further and Higher Education when it occasionally arises as a real option. But the option is a narrow one and very few of the kids we work with are placed to take it up. As far as photography itself is concerned and the kind of work we have been developing, it can also represent yet another closing down of growing interests and possibilities.

Seeking a social practice

Marco, one of the contributors to the exhibition 'Home, School, Work'[1] expressed his wish to keep doing photography with us after he left school,but he had no vocational interest in photography. He had left school for a Work Experience scheme and later YTS. Marco experienced this as leaving the frying pan for the fire. His disaffection with school turned to anger and boredom on YTS. He

A panel/montage which Marco prepared for the 'Home, School, Work' exhibition

began to take pictures of his days in the YTS workshops and to collect together the pictures he had taken at home over the previous years. He wanted to show what his real interests were and, as he put it, how useless his schooling had been to him. He wanted to return to school with a camera and retrospectively show how a lot of young people spent their days there. He spoke a lot about boredom, indiscipline, and conflict between groups at school, and about what other young people might learn from what he would show. He also wanted to confront an adult world of authority with his experience of their institutions. One day he visited our darkroom, after having taken photographs on a CND demo that weekend. He had the beginnings of an idea for a montage which would express his fears about nuclear war and what the future could be like. It was very difficult, in practical terms, for us to work with Marco on an individual basis. This is a general problem for a small group of teachers who are organised to work with groups. Our staffing and timetable cannot cope with the demands of individuals pursuing independent work at numerous points across a working week, which are determined by their availability. This was a very concrete example of the need for the extended and locally situated networks of institutions which we were looking to build. As it was we did our best to give Marco some time and free run of our resources. Eventually, on the basis of his evident continuing interest in photography and his quandary about a future, we negotiated and helped him make an application to an FE college. We helped put together a folio from his photographs and even found ourselves returning to old practices. We set him still lifes to draw and got him to fill a sketch book with drawings from observation and imagination. Marco duly got himself a place on a pre-foundation course in Art and Design, with a small maintenance grant and commitment to gaining an English

O-level or CSE in his first year. There could have been obvious benefits in this for Marco who had left school with there being no expectation on his own part and definitely not on his teachers', of him having any chance of vocational training in FE. But how did it serve to give Marco a structure in which to realise the interest which he had come to take in photography as a means both of exploring his identity and taking his social experience seriously? We cannot say in detail but we know that in broad terms photography became again an element within the initial stages of vocational specialism; a technical study with a range of prescribed formal effects to be rehearsed. Within the framework of the course he had embarked upon this would be inevitable and has its own rationale. This is not our immediate point of difficulty. The point is that a social practice is hived off as an area of study, once more to be a part of a syllabus. Photography and the experience he represented through it ceased to be the ground on which Marco met us. We sensed that he was unhappy. He may well have blamed us for finally bringing a working relationship to an end and shunting him back to the kind of educational context which he had always found so oppressive and meaningless. He certainly became more guarded in his relationship with us as we occasionally met in the neighbourhood. Photography was no longer a point of social exchange. On the last occasions that we met him it was to play pool in a local pub or a chance meeting in the street when he kept the talk firmly about the relative merits of the video hire shops in the area.

In the current context of youth unemployment, cuts in educational provision and the enforced free time for many young people, a job, and FE place, even an engrossing, albeit expensive, hobby have to be relatively good outcomes for kids we've worked with. But as we've seen, the question still stands. Where do young people break out of the practice of photography which fetishes the technical means and mystifies the products? What are the alternatives to the dominant institutions and the dominant routes through them?

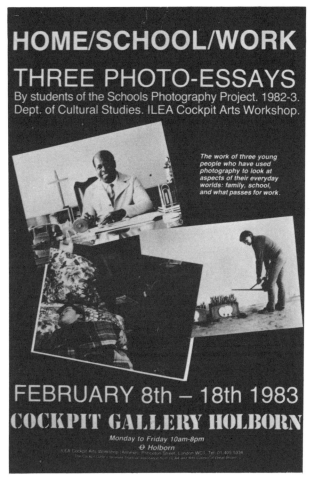

HOME/SCHOOL/WORK

THREE PHOTO-ESSAYS

By students of the Schools Photography Project. 1982-3.
Dept. of Cultural Studies. ILEA Cockpit Arts Workshop.

The work of three young
people who have used
photography to look at
aspects of their everyday
worlds: family, school,
and what passes for work.

FEBRUARY 8th – 18th 1983

COCKPIT GALLERY HOLBORN

Monday to Friday 10am-8pm
↔ Holborn

Cockpit Gallery poster

Critical routes through further education

Clearly some people use Further and Higher Education to undertake critical studies of culture and to acquire skills which they do not intend to use for dominant purposes. But these uses are rarely formalised into permanent courses and options. The radical and critical study option or course within the progressive college is always the result of a conjuncture between the intentions of a liberal management, the presence on a staff of radical or socialist teachers, and a student body looking for a relationship between their politics and their education. We could hardly hope to give an account of current forms of struggle over definitions of photographic practice in Further and Higher Education. But we mention the fact of such critical cultural processes taking place within dominant institutions of Further and Higher education because some young people who attend them do get involved in understanding practice and ideology. For working-class young people as a whole, however, this hardly constitutes an alternative to the institutions of work and leisure as places to have a relation to photography. This is because critical cultural studies is something that takes place a long way into competitive and selective institutions. In short, critical education is something which can usually only be encountered by individuals who are successfully pursuing educational advancement.

Some degree of continuity between establishing a photo practice within our approach and study within Further Education was probably experienced by another young man who contributed to 'Home, School, Work'.[1] It was largely the degree to which Yuk aspired throughout his school career and his work with us, to educational success, that can be seen to account for this. At the same time a reflexive practice of photography was always in an awkward tension with the need to fulfil dominant educational criteria. No doubt this tension still exists for him as he works through a course in Further Education, speaking as he does of the distinction between the requirements of the course and a more widely ranging practice of photography which he knows to exist.

Yuk came to us with a strong but as yet unformed vocational interest in photography. He carried out two years work with us as part of a timetabled school group. Photography was a special option within their GCE Art course. Yuk was a diligent and earnest pupil for whom a professional future in the Art and Design area was a long-term goal. He knew that this would not come easily, it was a highly competitive area and he was no academic high flyer. But he was

A photograph of Yuk, questionnaire and chart, used in a Schools Project about 'images of your future'

very tenacious and had made up his mind to compete on the terms offered. The technical competence and conventional range of his work was based in this vocational drive and his resolve to acquire skills. In the early days of project work, this same vocationally inflected view of photography created the tension we have referred to. We often sensed that he was bemused, not to say irritated at times, by the way that technical instruction and facilitation were linked in our approach to projects which centred him and his world as the content of photographs. Yuk would often attempt to reconcile this difficulty by doing all he could to translate projects into formal exercises. He would interpret an assignment to photograph his weekend into a careful study of the surfaces and patterns of light which fell across the balcony of his parent's flat. So often, Yuk's photographs would stand apart from those taken by the rest of his group. They were distinct in the way that he used the capacity of the photograph to render the symmetrical patterns, structures and surfaces of the visible world in a selective way which excluded any direct iconography or social connotation.

The work which he later carried out as an independent and self-organised project looked at his family's present way of life and their past in Hong Kong. He collected old family photographs, copied them and set them in front of his own image. He made a montage which represents his relationship to his family's past and his own early childhood in the British colony. In another panel he showed his present home in an inner city council flat, his mother's world, the family's affection for his small brother, and his parent's maintenance of their native culture.

A final panel concerned his father's world of work. In doing this work Yuk became involved in controlling the social power of photographs. Over a period of weeks Yuk struggled with the ways in which a combination of photographs and other material could be made to represent his father's difficult experiences as a railway porter during

Yuk's photograph of his father

Yuk's photograph of his young brother

Photo-montage by Yuk from the exhibition 'Home, School, Work'

IMAGES: PAST AND PRESENT

(Above and p. 122) Two panels by Yuk from the exhibition 'Home, School, Work'

the 1981 railway workers' strike. He was careful and respectful of his own feelings and confusions about the event and what could be shown in photographs. He thought about what they would mean to his family as a primary audience. He came to know and handle the power of representations. Within this project Yuk moved a long way from his earlier, more institutionally defined views about photography.

It was soon after this that he gained a place on a vocational Art and Design course, having used this work in his folder of application. For Yuk the world of dominant photographic education was something he entered with a sense of achievement. For him it was a fulfilment of a goal; he could readily accept its rationales and confidently expect its rewards in a professional future. But at the risk of overplaying our point, we still have to recognise that his option was a narrow one, open to only a few and, as Yuk himself can sense, involves a break or a limiting of an independent cultural practice.

It seems to us that, whether we like it or not, the established cultural and educational institutions through which young people might continue and extend a practice started with us are not organised with communities, collectives and groups in mind. In fact if we look beyond the points of access young people have to these institutions, to their position within them, we can see that individualism is there as the central logic. They are also competitive organisations. In one sense this is but a continuation of the institutional order of the school. Competitive examination will already have put the majority on the wrong side of entrance into Further and Higher Education. Courses within the colle-

ges are based upon competition for marks grades and status, however disguised, and finally upon competition for jobs. Even the camera club and the hobbyists don't escape competition. In fact they are often present in the acute form of club exhibitions where prizes, awards and commendations are competed for. Here the grading and judging of photographs is a popular aping of the status building of the great photographers, which in turn is a version of the artistic genius. It looks to us as if all the established institutions of photography reproduce the greater ideology of individualism through the lesser technical ideology of creativity. This is as true of the amateur and educational as it is of the professional and commercial.

Differences between community and school-based work

These thoughts led us to be interested in photographic projects with a more straight-forward relationship to communities. We attended regular, if infrequent, meetings where project workers would get together to share the problems and experience of doing photography with young people. What emerged for us was the determining effect of the initial institutional context and situation of the practice. If our practice was character-istically schoolish, then the community projects had the character and hallmark of com-muniteness. Much of this impression was explained simply as the differences in the material resources between projects; since all the community projects were operating on very low budgets there was a common cha-racter, the presentation of work. But beyond this initial observation more significant differences were noted between school and community-based work. The strongest observation was that photographic work undertaken by young people as part of school-work was more developed than that undertaken by similar young people working in community contexts. To community workers, our work with young people looked

highly structured. To us, the community photography looked informal and casual. It was recognised that in the school-based work themes and issues were followed through to more complex ideational and technical levels. In comparison the community-based work was recognised as more diverse and initial. This general observation of difference was important within the meetings because the community-based workers expressed it as the problem of achieving the conditions under which the work of young people could become more developed, whilst we expressed the problem of young people's work needing to have significance and currency beyond school. We were all recognising that institutional expectations, orientations and controls were highly determining upon the work young people do. In our different ways we all wanted to transform some of the established expectations of our working situations which were limiting its scope and currency. We wanted to extend the context in which young people were working.[2]

The 'Looking Out' exhibition

In a modest and still tentative way the workers meeting considered that it was within their scope to do something practical in respect of the context in which young people's existing work was seen and by which they see other work. This was discussed as the need to circulate the work of young people across projects, and to encourage young people beyond the immediate project to see photographic work. A London based open photographic exhibition for and involving young people was proposed for the summer of 1983, and was entitled 'Looking Out'. As the largest project represented at the meetings it was agreed that we were in a position to organise it. The exhibition was held at the Cockpit Gallery for three weeks in July and showed the work of fourteen projects. From the outset of organising 'Looking Out' it was recognised that the exhibition

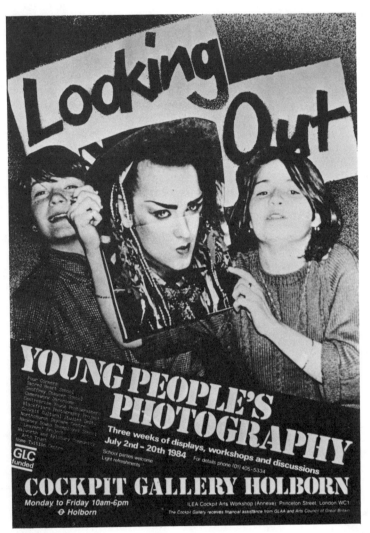

Cockpit Gallery poster

form was problematic, especially for working-class young people. We started from the premise that there is no easy route from the cultural worlds of working-class young people to the cultural assumptions and cultural hierachies contained in exhibiting photographs in a gallery. 'Looking Out' was seen as an initial meeting point from which we'd learn and from which contacts and further networks could be established.

All the time-honoured conventions by which the photographic community expresses its interests were made provisional in 'Looking Out'. We didn't expect a self-selecting audience to view the work and we didn't want or expect the privatised form of hushed viewing and informed chat at a private view. At the same time, we had no ready-made alternative youth version. We did have something like a private view when we chose one evening when most of the young photographers from the projects came with their workers. We had music, peanuts and soft drinks, which was conventional. We also had as much work of young people as we could find on the walls and laid out on tables. Fifty or sixty young people avidly consumed every last piece of work and were asking for more. In addition, we opened the studio for impromptu group sessions. The evening could be described by us as more of a workshop or open day, it had a vague relation to something approaching a performance although no one performed. That evening was 'Looking Out' as far as young people were concerned. The show continued and many adults saw it or came to the workers' seminars in which work with young people was discussed. For the young people, as they jostled home in the mini-bus or walked off in pairs to catch the bus, it had been a night up-town, a night out of area. We recognised before and after that few would have come without the organisation of the worker.

Overall the 'Looking Out' workers' meeting was encouraged by this first exhibition and as it resumed in the autumn of '83 there was enough enthusiasm to make 'Looking Out' an annual show. With more time it was thought that the exhibition form could be made to relate more closely to young people. They might be able to relate themes and issues in their work expressly for the exhibition. Workshops could become organised for different groups and on different aspects of practice. Also, and for CENTREPRISE and FOUR CORNERS[3] especially, young people could become more involved in the organisation and control of the exhibition. 'Looking Out '84' was held at the Cockpit Gallery, Holborn, in July. It was a more organised and extended event than the previous year and was, by common consent of the workers, less successful. It was over-organised and under-attended. Somewhere we'd lost the thread that the combined meeting was following, or it had been too frail to contain all the ambitions held for young people and snapped. In subsequent meetings during the winter of 1984, when future prospects were under consideration, the earlier guardedness had reappeared. Interest in a common, larger project was retreating not only through the qualified failure of the second 'Looking Out', but under all the combined pressures upon each

individual project; under competition for GLC grants and diverging sectional politics. The 'Looking Out' energy finally drained for us when CAMERAWORK,[4] which had been going through a period of internal reorganisation, came out and organised its own youth show without reference to 'Looking Out'. The tide of sectional interest was becoming overbearing.

Of all the many lessons learned and understandings made through the 'Looking Out' experience, the most illuminating and continuous for us concerned the situated nature of young people's photographic work. It seemed to us, watching those fifty young people excitedly viewing their own work on the walls, that more than anything else they were attempting to make concrete connections between what was depicted. They wanted to situate the photographs or collections of photographs. They scanned and searched for all the signs and clues as to the identify of those in the photos and where they were taken. This wasn't a total or exclusive mode of perception, but it was the most powerful and available way of socially valuing the work.

The Southwark Project

The attempt to situate our own practice with young people beyond school, yet in significant cultural contexts for them, constituted our second and parallel initiative to 'Looking Out'. Amongst other things the major practical work of 'Looking Out' was to create a London-wide network for young people's photographic work. In contrast, the Southwark Project aimed to create a network within part of a borough, Bermondsey, Peckham and Walworth. The Southwark Project was our attempt to locate the work we did with young people in school much closer to the patterns, venues, and occasions of everyday life. Like the 'Looking Out' meetings, this involved us in establishing and developing links with cultural projects and agencies operating within the same social and geogra-

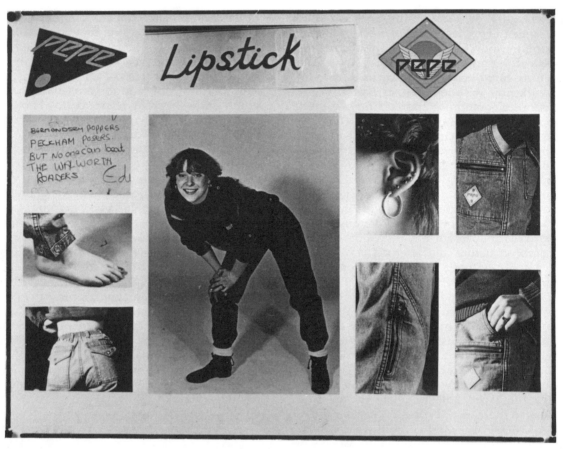

A panel by Donna Gill. Images of style and territory: the Walworth Roaders

phical areas as the schools we worked in. Similarly it required us to meet other cultural and education workers to discuss collaborations and common interests and to build practical links. Unlike the 'Looking Out' meetings the Southwark Project was more disparate from its inception and developed unevenly in response to specific collaborations between ourselves and one or other agency. In the end the Southwark Project also failed to unite interests across sites and institutions in any lasting way, and for similar reasons in the same period. The Southwark Project did contain fruitful collaborations and discussions, which in our view extends our understanding of the nature and difficulties of the continued need for a situated practice.

Practical collaborations — in Southwark

In the middle of Walworth, in the London Borough of Southwark, is the Aylesbury Estate. Its deck access blocks lie like a fleet at anchor. Gross and out of scale with the earlier environment, it is not liked by those who live on or near it. Yet there it sits and there it will stay. It has been the subject of architectural awards, sociological research and TV documentaries. It is too new and houses too many for anything to happen to it for a long time. It stretches from the Wal-

The Aylesbury Estate, Southwark, friends and activities. A panel/montage by Donna Gill

worth Road and the Old Kent Road as its east and west boundaries and from the Elephant and Castle and Burgess Park from the North to the South. The park has been growing like a patchwork quilt and now stretches south to the North Peckham Estate. It is the pride of the GLC parks development programme and has recently sported a boating and a fishing lake. The other important part of the picture is the local market down East Lane that runs untroubled by the looming Aylesbury Estate, which stands at the far end of the street. Many of the young people whom we teach live on the Aylesbury Estate, or know

Photography group montage

Photography group montage, using group studio shots ·

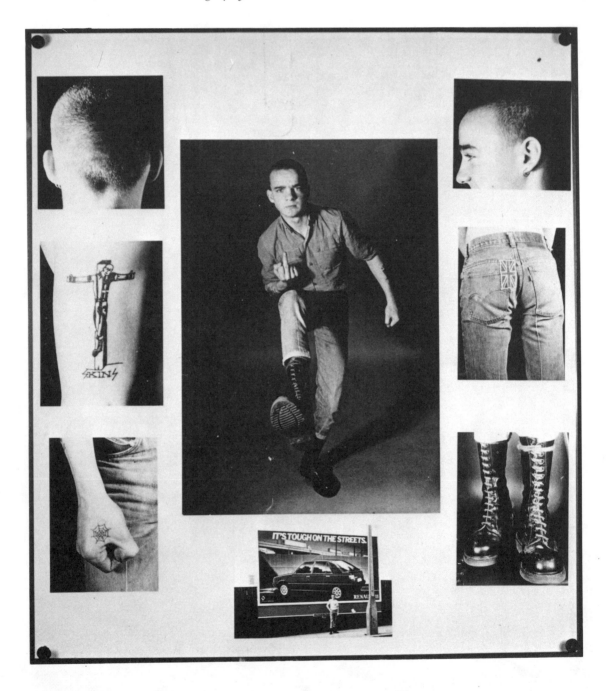

Pete, who is seen as a member of the group depicted in previous pages, produced his own panel, above. While Donna worked on the territorially-based style of the Walworth Road. Pete represented the more universalised, sub-cultural iconography of the Skinhead

Cover of the 'Glue Sniffin' pamphlet, a collaboration between Brendan and Francis Henley, the Chaplin Centre, Walworth, and Aylesbury Community Arts Trust and the Cockpit (see page 132)

someone who does. Donna Gill's work on page 127 shows something of the character of the Aylesbury buildings. On the Aylesbury Estate there is a day care centre currently called the Chaplin Centre – Charlie used to live just round the corner. Four years ago Steve Miller, who had worked part-time for the Department of Cultural Studies, got a job as the teacher there to provide the legally required education for young people obliged by the courts or the Social Services Department to attend the centre. Subsequently we were able to arrange a secondment for Steve Miller to work at the Cockpit and for us to do some work with him at the Chaplin Centre.[5] It was the work we did with Steve and the young people from Chaplin that had the most located and situated character and whose themes related closely to life in and around the Aylesbury. Also on the Aylesbury, in close proximity to the Chaplin Centre, is the Walworth and Aylesbury Community Arts Trust, WACAT for short. At the time of our collaboration with Steve and the young people from Chaplin, Steve was in contact with the photography worker at WACAT.[6] Together they had done one or two introductory pieces of work with Steve's group. One of these had been to photograph Brendan and Francis Healey around the sheds where they had been glue sniffing. In conjunction with the photos, Brendan and Francis spoke and wrote about their experience of glue sniffing. Steve worked with them to combine the photos and commentary in the production of a pamphlet, the cover of which we reproduce here. The pamphlets were produced and sold at 35p and the money was used to pay a court fine of £50 which had been imposed on them.

At the time of this production there was a great deal of concern about the emergence of industrial solvent sniffing and its effects on young people of school age. The concern was typically and quickly fashioned into prohibitions and warnings rather than into understanding and experience. Young people were interested and dire warnings only served to increase the curiosity of those most socially susceptible to trying it out. The pamphlet aimed at communication and understanding which was close to young people's interest and experience. The pamphlet sold quickly and has been subsequently used as a text in one of the schools we teach in. Shortly after, another pamphlet was produced along similar lines, the important difference being that it was a fictional account of one outcome of heroin used by a young person. This was undertaken by two young women working with Steve and ourselves both in the local area and at the Cockpit centre. Again it was printed, this time as an A4 pamphlet, and sold by the girls and local agencies. Moving on from glue sniffing, the Aylesbury Estate has emerged as one of the areas where Heroin is easily and cheaply available for young people and where, for a depressing range of reasons, some working-class young people have now a developed habit. The pamphlet of the two young women speaks from the edge of that experience in relationship to a cultural interest. It is close work. It's form is popular and valued. The issue it deals with is current. For the producers this combines to give force and meaning to the practical production. They acquire and practice skills they otherwise resist within school. They value the production sufficiently to follow through each stage and when it is complete as a product they go out and sell it. And of course it sells because it has popular currency in its obvious form and context. Such pamphlets continue to have interest beyond the immediate area of their production and outside the specific locale to which they refer. But the primary achievement is that they are valued and do achieve effective transmission precisely in the immediate territory of their producers. They are small success stories and as such encourage us to attempt similar and continuing work.

Yet more references to 'Madness' among the images photographed on a young person's bedroom wall (see page 74)

5

Future Directions

In marking out the limits and possibilities of the 'Looking Out' organisation and the Southwark Project initiative at the end of the last chapter, we have also reached the end of the substantial account of our project. It remains the task of this final chapter to summarise the account and offer a conclusion. We have, eventually, chosen to do this in a way which stresses the underlying educational argument which runs throughout the account. This constitutes our summary and from there we go on to make a further set of general points in the style of a series of recommendations for further practice. In between the summary and recommendations we have felt it necessary to offer a brief description of some other aspects of our wage labouring context which relate to the youth photography projects and which have a bearing upon how the reader can locate the overall account and assess our concluding remarks. Altogether, then, we have gone for a conclusion which we intend to be of practical use to workers and those interested in working within the field of contemporary popular cultural studies.

Throughout the account of our practical photography work we continually raise broader issues relating to our understanding of the value of the practice to young people. This extends from the consideration of the cultural formation of our own generational ideas and interests, to how we understand the social worlds of young people, through to how they variously respond to and value the practice we offer. The issues raised, the problems we define and the descriptions we give are connected by a contextual argument about the culturally oppressive nature of educational institutions for working-class

young people and their response in the form of popular cultural resistance. The argument is ultimately a historical, political and situated one and does, we believe, lead to a practical basis for working positively with dissaffected youth. But, as we say, the argument is given in the overall text and many of its features remain implicit. The following summary of the account, chapter by chapter, presents the arguments more clearly.

The argument

Chapter 1

We began by giving some time to a consideration of the period preceding that of the actual project. We stress our own educational background in the context of the expansion of Further and Higher Education in the 1960s, and how this led to increased opportunities for upper working-class students. We characterise this period of expansion in broader terms as a development of a social-democratic concensus in parliamentary politics and in education as the emergence of a liberal progressivism offering space for reform. We say that a general liberalisation of course content and teaching methods took place across the field of education. Within this context we locate our specific reforming project around the democratisation of cultural practice in relationship to a critique of Art Education and Art Teacher Training. Our central interpretation of the cultural democratisation argument revolved around the need for a valuation of popular forms and popular experience. It led us eventually to centre on the particular experience and culture of working-class youth and their compulsory schooling.

From there we point out that our photo practice with youth was subsequently carried out in a different period of worsening conditions and ideological attacks upon post-war democratic gains. In education we witnessed ten years of cuts and closures and the effects of growing youth unemployment. We note that these changes had outcomes both upon the way in which our initiative was taken up and valued and crucially on the position of working-class young people. The rejection of progressivism in education in favour of traditional categories and virtues, together with the massive increase in youth unemployment, sharpened and highlighted a whole set of issues around the position of youth in society. We illustrate this by showing how the dominant representation of youth continues to construct youth as both the mythical carrier of freedom and as a threat to settled society. The image of youth as an uncivilised element is used as part of a moral panic which hides an increasingly authoritarian and violent policing policy directed in part at the young unemployed themselves, and especially at the hardest hit amongst them, black youth. Somewhere in relation to these dominant stereotypes we recognise that young people have to make sense of themselves in society. We point out that an important context for 'making sense' is precisely in the area of popular representation.

At the end of Chapter 1 we speak of the major theme of our projects and of this book as the connection between the sense young people make of their experience of photography as a means of representation and of schooling as a site of practice. We locate our project very precisely in relationship to the larger crisis facing young people. First, we recognise that they experience crisis in the heightened form of a 'broken' transition from school to work. Secondly, we note that transition is the period when future identities are explored, confirmed or rejected. Thirdly, that photography has both a dominant function and popular currency which significantly relates to youth cultural practice.

Chapter 2

The position of schooling in our account is, above all, given by its compulsory nature. So, as much as we continually recognise real problems in trying to establish an informal popular practice in a formal unpopular institution, we also recognise that there is no other alternative which involves the majority of young people.

In Chapter 2 we point out by our own example that it is possible to establish relatively independent practical photography projects within a number of school sites. Whilst it is clearly important to be concerned with how such projects are rationalised as part of schooling, our point is that it is more important to be concerned with how young people take them up and the further possibilities contained in their response. Having outlined how it is that young people are readily prepared to engage with a practice which offers them control around definitions, we say that it becomes important to look closely at their responses. Throughout the entire account we lay great stress on the fact that in order to observe young people it is necessary to construct a framework for understanding. It was through such a process of observation that we discovered the inadequacy of an early model which distinguished young people's response to school on the basis of conformity/resistance, (earoles/lads). Our own understanding which we illustrate in the discussion of how some young people take up a practice of photography, is that such a distinction does not account for passive forms of resistance, for instance. It was by the same process that we were able to see that the school/home dichotomy is more complex and less distinct as young people go through the school day. We say, for instance, that much is carried on in school which refers to worlds out of school. We say that family and, for some young people, a sense of belonging to an area or territory are important factors in how they negotiate schooling. We argue that normally the world beyond school, the contingent reality of everyday life, remains an unacknowledged force within schooling. Yet this wider reality has a pacing and shaping effect on school. The daily conflicts and antagonisms, the moods, incidents and social relationships that are established owe much to the world beyond school. We make the point that schooling is unable to relate positively to this everyday reality, in part because it is experienced by teachers as a threat to the order of school and because where it is valued there are so little forms for its expression. We demonstrate that the photo practice makes many aspects of everyday reality visible and potentially public, and hence possible to engage with.

Chapter 3

We continue this line of argument in Chapter 3 by relating what young people express and explore through photography to their contemporary cultural forms of resistance. First, we locate the specific oppression of the young people we've worked with in the context of the economic exploitation and social oppression of the working class. Secondly, we point out that working-class young people experience oppression in the specific and differential ways that they are made subordinate. Hence we identify racism and sexism as general systems of oppression. Our argument then suggests that resistance is also experienced by young people as part of their specific and differential cultures, and therefore that young people learn to resist as much as they learn subordination. Popular resistance is, we say, a stance towards conditions of pervasive oppression. For oppressed groups resistance is part of the active process of cultural empowerment. Hence forms of resistance are closely related to forms of identity. In this last respect we point out that the 'exploration' of dominant identities (subordinate positions) contains possibilities for resistance.

Having centred resistance as a key to much

that working-class young people express about their everyday life, we locate a central set of difficulties concerning our attempt to establish educational practices with them. We identify the central issue as the recognition and experience that the young people we've worked with do not give up their resistant stances, outlooks and practices just because they like doing photography. Or, more seriously, they can't suspend resistance since it is constitutive of their identities. Equally we can't easily identify the interests we have for them as if there were a 'given' channel of communication and a 'common' set of values. We argue that the position of a shared project has to be struggled for. This is discussed in terms of a method and style of teaching and we recognise there is no easy path and no magical solutions in such an undertaking and that many 'closures' are possible. We move the argument on by saying that this central difficulty is kept in place by existing institutional arrangements and that there are therefore severe limits to working within school. We suggest that alternatives have to be sought.

Chapter 4

In the first half of Chapter 4 we demonstrate how the existing institutional arrangements conspire against the development of a social and cultural practice of photography. We show that the available institutional routes through which young people can pursue or maintain an interest in photography require marked accommodations to dominant purposes. We also point out that these accommodations are, on the whole, ones that working-class young people are not able to make. We do, however, recognise that it is important to encourage individuals to pursue the available routes where they exist as possibilities. But, in terms of cultural practice, we argue that it is important for teachers, lecturers, cultural workers *et al.* to explore unofficial networks and collaborations in order to support and extend their practice. We argue that it is important to retain control and independence for the practice. We back this up by giving two examples of where we have attempted to work in relationship to broader networks and collaborations. The first was on the basis of a community of interest in photography and the second was where we worked in a geographical community. We discuss the strengths and weaknesses of both models and conclude that whilst we don't accept a view that there is one correct strategy, it is work which manages to stay close to local communities and interests that has the strongest chance of success.

The basis of the practical work at the Cockpit

This account has followed the developments of youth photography projects which we ran from the Department of Cultural Studies of the Cockpit Arts Workshop. Photography projects were the centre of our work but by no means took up all our working time. On average, about two-thirds of our week was spent on work directly related to the teaching projects. The remainder of our time was spent in administration,working with other teachers or students in Higher Education, writing, publishing and producing exhibitions. All this work was connected to the youth photography projects. In general, it was that part of our own work concerned to establish networks and extend the field of interest. It does, therefore, have a bearing upon our argument and conclusion.

For the last three years we have been writing this account alongside the projects. As we consign these last words much has already changed and is still changing in the cluster of institutional factors which gave rise to the projects in the first place. By our own cultural analysis nothing stays still and our own project is no exception. The conjucture which brought together a particular group of people at a particular time and in relation to a particular set of ideas has already dissolved, leaving us the ideas and practices in a more fragmented set of relationships. It is important for this to be said

for the very reason that we don't offer this account as the basis for a practice, nor do we propose the Cockpit as a model institution. What we hope will flow from our example is an orientation towards cultural practice and a sharper interest in the possibilities of popular contemporary cultural practices. It is our view that whilst the pedagogy we developed is not reproduceable under the conditions of most other educational venues, the concepts, aims and general approach are transferable to a variety of cultural contexts.

Arts Workshops arose in much more generous and buoyant times than those we are currently facing. Those that do survive are continually dogged by a perpetual cycle of financial insecurity. The Cockpit has always been unique in the benefits that accrue from having been fully funded by an education authority. This is indisputably the basis upon which our six years' work rest. The Cockpit as a whole still has a lively and developing programme of Arts work with young people in London and should be supported against the current threats to reduce its staffing. In relation to our own programme of work with schools, it is also the case that one-off projects are not a substitute for general provision in full-time schooling. Only a tiny fraction of young people in London have had the opportunity to work on our highly resourced projects. Cultural Studies has, we think, a much large contribution to make to schooling in general. This is why we think it important to make reference here to the wider project of the Department of Cultural Studies from which the specific photographic projects were undertaken. Our 'licence' to innovate carried with it the responsibility to report on our findings. This is why, prior to this account,we have published four separate descriptions of projects between ·1978 and 1985. We also took this responsibility to mean establishing a centre of interest, practical cultural studies projects and a focus for the issues raised relating to the culture and education of young people.

A journal

Publishing has been an important means of achieving both these aims. The flagship of the department's publishing enterprise has been the journal *Schooling and Culture*, which was founded in 1978 with the express purpose of offering description and analysis of cultural and educational practice relating to young people. Producing a termly journal within a teaching department was hard work, particularly since it involved practical production and distribution. Under the strain imposed *Schooling and Culture* dropped to a biannual publication in 1981, and in the face of the classic financial difficulty of limited cash flow has been suspended since the summer of 1984, after fourteen issues.[1] Interest in the journal has not declined, however, and it is ironic that as our ability to produce it decreased, demand has taken a reverse course. At present we receive around five new enquiries per week and as many in back issue orders. *Schooling and Culture*[1] aimed to constitute a readership from within the teaching professions. As such the majority of published writing was either analysis of the function of the system of education or examples of what we considered good practice with young people. As the editorial group our concern was to keep the journal close to the everyday realities and concerns of working-class young people and what it was possible to achieve with them. This latter aspect did lead to the occasional publication of students' work, but this was very much in the context of teaching examples. The stronger example of publishing students' photo-text work comes in the one off pamphlets that were produced as part of the projects. They were always local productions, sold locally and used in local schools. We produced comparatively few pamphlets and we have sited them earlier in the account as examples of what is possible, rather than pointing to a developed system of youth publishing.

Exhibitions

The better example of a developed system of publishing comes with the production of exhibitions. The Cockpit Gallery developed from two sources. The first and conventional was its basis as the theatre foyer exhibition space in the main Cockpit building. The second was a need, growing out of the projects, for exhibiting the work of young people or work which was thought of interest to them. With the department's move to new premises in 1978 the present gallery was founded. The gallery was originally staffed and organised from within the teaching team. As interest and demand were stimulated it became obvious that additional staffing would be needed and grant applications were made, initially to the Great London Arts Association for part-time administrative help. It had never been our intention to establish just a gallery, in the sense of pictures on walls. The basis of our interest was similar to that of publishing the journal. We were interested in distribution networks; ways of creating the channels of communication we saw as necessary to connect the scattered interests across different educational locations. To this end the exhibition touring system was a much more important aspect of the gallery project than the gallery exhibition programme. It was via publicising and touring exhibitions that young people's work could be seen outside the local context in which it was produced. By 1982 the gallery project had developed to the point where it could be considered as a separate organisation from the teaching team of the department. With GLC funding the gallery gained three full-time staff at the beginning of 1983. The department's relationship to it became one of liaison and collaboration where the gallery staff established their own policy and programme. The demand for exhibition loan within the touring system is currently greater than the staff can cope with. To meet this demand a financial growth is needed which looks impossible in the face of an uncertain future for the entire project with the abolition of the GLC.[2]

Both the journal and the gallery grew out of the needs related to developments in the teaching programme. We saw them as necessary forms for the dissemination of material and for the creation of networks of interest. Between 1979 and 1983 they were related to the overall work of the department on a collective basis. Over this same period of time the department made two other arrangements which had important outcomes on the direction and force of the photography projects. Firstly, in 1979, we applied for and were successful in getting a photographer-in-residence post from GLAA. Our proposal for a residency involved collaboration and integration in the teaching projects, whilst maintaining a distinction between the role of photographer and the role of teacher. This proved highly successful and, of course, added to the number of people working and the amount of work we could take on. The second arrangement also concerned staffing. With the secondment of a member of the department to the GLC's Art Committee as a policy advisor, we were able to arrange a secondment for a teacher we had been working with in Southwark. This increased the profile of our work in Southwark and eventually led to the establishment of the Southwark Project plan. Taken together these arrangements gave additional scope to the teaching projects.

In the same way that we had considered the journal and the gallery as logical extensions of our programme of practical photographic work, we regarded the residency and secondment as furthering our aims. In particular we saw the residency as an opportunity to discuss our ideas of photography as a cultural practice with a person coming from a 'photographic' background. We saw the secondment as an opportunity to develop practical work in a closer relationship to a local area and to explore the concept of territory. The Southwark Project aimed to bring the teaching projects, our interest in cultural networks, publishing projects and touring

exhibitions together in the location with which we had the most contact. In the pilot year we met and worked with existing community arts projects and expanded the number of local schools we worked in. We held Southwark Project workers' meetings and planned for a newsheet to be produced. The possibility of establishing a local photo archive was discussed with various agencies and proposals for funding were written.[3]

So by 1982 the work we had started four years earlier in the pilot year of the Schools Photography Project had grown considerably in both its scale and scope. The gallery, the journal, the residency and the secondment had all been promoted by the aim of establishing a means of cultural expression with and for young people. Establishing these forms and arrangements had taken considerable organisational effort. Administering and maintaining them required a regular portion of time. Keeping a balance between the competing demands of the teaching projects, the journal and the gallery finally became an impossible task for three full-time workers.

Since 1983 there has been a steady fragmentation of the various strands of work which developed from a collective project and a reforming of interests and aims. The gallery and touring system is currently an autonomous project funded by GLC with specific collaboration with the department. *Schooling and Culture* is suspended, pending more funds. The residency concluded in 1985 having been continued for two years on ILEA part-time hours. The Southwark Project has devolved into a secondment of another member of the department as an education development worker at a new Urban Studies Centre in Peckham. In effect, the larger unified project of the Department of Cultural Studies reached its peak in 1982–3 and since that time has been fragmenting and reforming. The work described in this book belongs to that period. The future direction of such work at the Cockpit is largely unknown as this point. What is known and hence possible to discuss in general terms is the broad outline of a youth cultural practice arising out of our work to date.

Recommendations

A *situated politics*

The perspectives which underpin the argument in this account and which informed the development of the projects are broadly socialist in character. The specific alignments and commitments of individuals who have worked upon the project, including ourselves, have had a bearing upon the development of the work. Most often this has been in the characteristic form of disagreements about the broader strategies to which our practice could be attached. At other times differences have emerged at the closer level of how we both viewed and valued working-class and youth culture. These were always arguments about what was progressive and they continue in the very current and sharp form of debates about the sexist and racist character of popular cultural responses. This is a continuous and ongoing part of the work. But it is clear to us that the practice could never have been established if differences had been raised to the level of so called 'principled politics'. We very strongly reject the approach where the world has to fit the current official pronouncement of the 'progressive principle'. For socialist teachers especially this is always disarming, for it is the case, and has been for a very long time, that working-class young people are at the most confused end of politics and ideology. The development of a genuinely popular politics will have to stay close to their responses and many of these contain things that are dominant and reactionary. In saying this we have not thrown away (our) socialist principles, but are stressing a more general, deeper historical sense of what these principles are in a commitment to change. We would like to think that the educational practice we have developed is related to the popular traditions of independent working-class and progressive education, where a common (practical) sense can still be a starting point. For it is also the case that young people express much that is positive and progressive but you will only hear this if you are in a relationship with them. Our final recommendations are committed precisely in these terms; to establish conditions and develop practices which do justice to the progressive instincts of youth.

Future promise and directions

Youth

We urge that any project or programme of cultural and educational work with young people consider the following:

1. *Young people have important things to say*

It is central to listen to and take seriously what they say. This is not simply a straightforward process of social exchange as in 'all right I'm listening, what are you saying?' It cannot be expected that they will value your forms of speech, discussion, etc. Ways have to be found to encourage their expression at every level of exchange from casual conversation to group discussion and decision-making. This is as much about creating the conditions in which they can speak as in the need for girls-only activities, for instance.

2. *We need to learn from young people*

We believe that it is essential for workers to develop frameworks for understanding the worlds of young people. We think that projects should include research, discussion and analysis of the conditions, interests and expressions of young people. This should be carried out in trust with their knowledge, consent and, where possible, participation.

3. *Young people can take responsibility*

Within projects they can become independent and self-organising. It is important to include them in the organisation of work programmes, schedules and arrangements and to give them real responsibilities for carrying out work.

4. *Young people want to be included*
Work should take place in relationship to real interests and contexts which are developed in consultation with young people.

5. *Young people want to learn*
Whilst always working with specific practices, it is important to keep an open mind about what can be the subject of enquiry and how work might develop.

Photography

As any reader who has some experience in using photography will know, it is a very powerful tool. It is one of a number of light recording mediums at the very centre of developed communication systems. As such, and as we have argued throughout this account, its power is not lost on young people. What is less clear is how it can be used in education over a range of subjects and practices. From all that we have said we recommend photography because of the following.

1. *Photography can be a sustained educational practice*
Photography can be organised as a regular practical activity involving the acquisition of continuous developing skills. At the same time, it can be used in relationship to diverse interests. In this sense it can be a sustained practice over both long periods of time and intense amounts of time.

2. *Photography can achieve complex communication*
We are all sophisticated receivers and viewers of cultural broadcasting and young people are no exception. The photographic film or video image, in juxtaposition with the spoken or printed word, is the basis of the major convention of contemporary communication. Through the various forms and uses of this convention complex cultural messages are relayed. Still photography has a number of forms which achieve complexity in constructing meanings. The skills to manipulate photographic conventions can be readily acquired by young people.

3. *Photography has cultural reach, expressivity and popularity*
Photography is, as we have argued, a popular cultural practice. Its popularity especially recommends it as an educational practice for young people. This is particulary the case for young people who do not relate to or value the unpopular practice of writing. Photography is also a powerful and available form of cultural and social expressivity with significant reach into both the public and private realms.

For these reasons photography is a powerful and educational means of cultural practice. For it to be relevant and related to working-class young people it also needs the following conditions.

1. *Photography needs to be situated*
Projects based on photography need to be closely related to the lives and interests of the users. Projects should be popular and available and part of the overall cultural landscape.

2. *Photography needs to be sustained*
Photography is capable of forming a sustained practice and it needs extended time if complex communication is to be achieved. This most often requires organisational work to maintain resources and funds but it also involves having the 'right' purpose for the work.

3. *Photography needs to be related*

Photography shouldn't turn in on itself or be reduced to a single practice. It is important to work with the mobile possibilities of the medium. It is important to realise its connections with all the allied reprographic forms of print since these enlarge circulation and forms.

4. *Photography should be reflexive*

Projects based on practical photography should in our view be responsive to the local cultural context in which they take place. Links should be made with other agencies, sites and individuals. Projects should involve more than photography in the sense that it is important to have a means of critical reflection in what is being produced.

Institutions

One of the overriding views of this account is that most youth institutions reproduce more than they transform. From this perspective we have argued that a disproportionate effort is required in establishing the conditions for a practice to occur. Inevitably this means negotiations with existing institutions. As we have pointed out, we don't have a special fondness for secondary schooling and recognise that there are enormous limits and restrictions in working within their regime. We have also argued that to ignore the institution of school when considering youth practice is a serious mistake. School as a site has to be taken on board for the following reasons:

1. However, unpopular schools are with young people, they are compelled to attend them for a considerable period of their lives and for the majority of the working day. So it is important to orientate practice to school even if only to negotiate from within it for working in other sites. It is simply the place to meet youth.

2. School is the institution *par excellence* where the assumption and expectation that learning takes place is located. However much we may doubt schools' ability to achieve significant learning or reject what it teaches, the conventional expectation that something can be learned is an important prerequisite.

3. In the above respect schools legitimate activity. Again we may not like the context of legitimation or its dominant form in the examination system, but again cultural practice has to negotiate some form of credibility in order to establish itself and reproduce its practice.

4. Schools contain resources, energy and skills which can be argued for a cultural practice.

Having noted what we take as the base line in relating to school as the site for cultural practice, what could be called the 'positive' side of the account, it is also important to state the 'negative' balance.

1. Schools divide the working day into portions of time which make little sense to sustained practice. The timetable is an inflexible arrangement of the working week which is difficult to adjust to relatively mobile and spontaneous demands.

2. The social relations of school reinforce hierarchical power and control, and work against self-organisation.

3. The structure of the curriculum vests authority in the teacher and the subject which does not encourage students taking responsibility for their own learning.

4. The underlying and dominant epistemology of knowledge denies students own knowledge and experience as a basis for learning.

To compete against the formidable established structure of power the following conditions should be argued for:

1. *Block timetabling* – to achieve reasonable periods of time in which to undertake serious and sustained work.

2. *Team-teaching* – so that skills can be shared and so that planning and evaluation can take place.

3. *Shared resources* – to ensure the maximum access to equipment and the necessary amount of consumable materials. This includes arguing for a budget.

4. *Autonomy* – to define the course of study, its aims and methods and the appropriate forms of assessment.

5. *Preparation time* – to gain a high level of achievement in each working session, to analyse results and collaborate with other agencies.

These basic conditions would apply equally to the establishment of a social practice of photography in any institution. It is interesting to note that many of these conditions are met on degree courses anyway, and some of them are present within primary schooling. Why not then in the secondary sector? However, overall we would argue that it is important in organising cultural work to think more in terms of a practice which spans sites, which is potentially multi-institutional.

To this end we urge those who organise from a school base to make every effort to form links with other cultural agencies which operate in the locality of the school in order that:

1. Work can be circulated beyond the school.

2. Real audiences for work can be constructed.

3. Other sources of experience within the community can be related to the practice.

This is, of course, a two-way process where other cultural agencies should be encouraged into the school and supported by it. In order for something resembling exchange to take place, it is necessary to create openings for outside agencies to use school resources and to propose joint work. Trade unions, voluntary organisations and cultural associations, as well as other institutions within the local authority, all have a relationship to education and young people and are amenable to concrete proposals. In short, if you want to work with working-class young people the starting-point of practice will most often be within institutions they are obliged to attend. The construction of that practice should involve the development of and participation within a wider cultural network.

Notes and References

1 Youth, Photography and Education

1. We would like to acknowledge the early support and teaching of Nick Wayte, a pychologist and poet who developed courses in critical social theory at Gloucestershire College of Art in the late sixties.
2. Subsequently much of this work has become incorporated into modern art as a critical 'ism' and now well may be seen in Bond Street or the South Bank.
3. In the early seventies adventure playgrounds and summer holiday play schemes often became the site for visual art and theatre projects of a temporary nature.
4. In particular CCCS Working Papers; *Resistance Through Rituals* and *On Ideology*.
5. Dick Hebdige, *Subculture: The Meaning of Style* (Methuen, 1979).
6. The hostility had two elements: (1) a feeling that our work undermined the 'intuitive' basis of creativity; and (2) that it was introducing politics into non-political education.
7. Douglas Lowndes and Alan Horrox's *Viewpoint*, made for Thames TV, was a particularly striking series about the media made for school (1978). It was withdrawn by Thames after Thames Director's deemed it 'political'.
8. See in particular CSE Media Studies syllabi which attempt to be critically 'objective' about media industries.
9. See also *Schooling and Culture* (issues 12/13) for our analysis of the role of the MSC.
10. Jo Spence also explores the ideological narratives of advertising in the exhibition *Family, Phantasy and Photography* (Cockpit Gallery, 1981).
11. During the pilot year of the Schools Photography Project we relied on sympathetic teachers to find legitimate ways of making links between their timetabled subjects and our courses. In Mark Dukes's case the link was made possible by Robin Collingwood, who was working in the Art Department at Tulse Hill School.
12. Style charts were temporary wall charts made with specific groups; we did produce a duplicated grid which project members could fill in themselves (see Mark Dukes illustrations, pp. 24–5).
13. Dave Hampshire worked as a Photographer-in-residence for the Department of Cultural Studies from 1979 until March 1986, both full- and subsequently part-time. He is most associated with the project and exhibition *Our Way of Rockin* (Cockpit Gallery, 1983).
14. The snapshot has been held to be a dominant, uncritical and non-aesthetic form of the photograph.
15. See *Resistance Through Rituals* (CCCS, 1976).

2 Photography as a Cultural Practice

1. For further discussion about the place of photography in schools see A. Dewdney and M. Lister, *Using Photography in Schools* (Cockpit Gallery, 1985).
2. This exercise is a simple version of the much more developed work of Jo Spence and Rose Martin which they call 'photo-therapy'.
3. Centreprise is a long-standing community publishing and literacy project based in Hackney, London. Ken Worpole was closely associated with its development as a prodigious publisher of working-class writing.
4. Judith Williamson, *Decoding Advertisements* (Cockpit Gallery, 19??).
5. Claire Grey, *Teaching Photography – A History of Photographic Work at Sacred Heart School* (Photography in Education, 1980) talks about the gendered nature of young people's choice of photographic subject.
6. Andrew Dewdney and Colin St Leger, *On Yer Bikes Boys, Boys' Pursuits and Understanding the Making of Men* (Cockpit Gallery, 1986) talks about photographic practice and deconstructing the dominant representation of men.
7. See also Yuk Man's photo-essay in *Home, School, Work* (exhibition Dept of Cultural Studies, 1983), and Adrian Chappell in *Gender and Generation* (Macmillan, 1984).
8. *Our Way of Rockin* (exhibition, Cockpit Gallery, 1983).
9. Paul Willis, *Learning to Labour* (Saxon House, 1977).

3 Cultural Resistance and Cultural Expansion

1. See, for example, the Inner London Education Authority adopted report, *Improving Secondary Schools*, by D. Hargreaves (1983) and the ILEA initiative documents on race, sex and class.
2. For evidence of the history of young people and criminal sub-cultures in South London, see C. Rook, *Hooligan Nights* (Oxford University Press, 1979).
3. See A. McRobbie, *Resistance Through Rituals* (1976) and C. Griffin, *Typical Girls* (Routledge, 1985).
4. The *Style* exhibition was never produced but student's work from the same school provided the basis for the *Being at School* exhibition, done in conjunction with Ian Sillett from Geoffrey Chaucer School (Cockpit Gallery, 1984).

4 Developing, Photo-Practice: Social Actions and Institutions

1. *Home, School, Work*, three photo-essays by students of the Schools Photography Project (Dept of Cultural Studies, 1983).
2. The Department ran the 'Looking Out' exhibition and workers' meetings in 1983 and 1984. The meetings were a continuation of a series of photography workers' meetings originally organised by Camerawork which had lapsed.
3. Four Corners is a film collective based in East London.
4. Camerawork, London-based photography project, one of the largest and most influential in the late seventies. Camerawork had been responsible for organising a London-based photography workers' meeting which was taken over by the Cockpit when it lapsed. Camerawork participated in 'Looking Out' and it was surprising that it should organise a group-based youth and photography show without reference to the Looking Out organisation.
5. Steve Miller worked for the Department on a full-time secondment basis for two years.
6. Walworth and Aylesbury Community Arts Trust ran a photography project in conjunction with a Print shop. We collaborated with the Trust during the period of Steve Miller's secondment. The photography workers at that time were Jo Barnett and Rob Hills.

5 Future Directions

1. *Schooling and Culture* was the journal of the Department from 1978 until 1984, when after Issue 14 it was suspended. The title 'Schooling and Culture' has been retained for an occasional publication series and back issues are still available.
2. Since the abolition of the GLC the Gallery project has become an independent trust and has temporary funding from the Richmond scheme, the GLAA and the London Borough of Camden, whilst retaining the free use of an ILEA building for the financial year 1986–87.
3. Aspects of the Southwark Project have been continued in Southwark with the secondment of Adrian Chappell from the Department of Cultural Studies to the Willowbrook Urban Studies Centre in Peckham.

Acknowledgements

The authors wish to thank the Arts Council for its financial assistance in the development of this book and towards the cost of the extensive photographic material included.

Acknowledgements also to:

all of the young people who worked on projects with us and who knew how to make work so enjoyable.

the many ILEA teachers who enabled us to work with their pupils and gave us support, especially: Alf Bradley, Norma Dews, Heather Flint, Chris Fruin, Bob Hills, Maggie Murray, John Stevens, Martin Sohn-Retel, and Dave Russell.

Dave Hampshire and Steve Miller, who carried out much of the work with us and whose skills, arguments, and energy were vital.

Robin Collingwood, Claire Grey, Colin St Leger and Ian Sillet whose ideas, involvement and interest made the work possible.

Adrian Chappell and Alan Tompkins, our co-workers in the Cockpit Department of Cultural Studies, and Alec Davison and Stuart Bennett for the spaces they created and defended.

our partners and children for roles that are hard to qualify.

Jo Spence for reading an early draft and being enthusiastic and supportive of the need to publish an account of the work.

A further special thanks to Claire Grey and Steve Miller for their invaluable hard work with paste-up and artwork.

A. D.
M. L.